Winning Online Instruction

Winning Online Instruction provides concise, pragmatic solutions to common challenges and demands that higher education faculty face in teaching online. This book's unique question-and-answer format allows readers to easily identify the issues important to them, spanning online formats and teaching methods, course development and technology woes, student motivation and engagement, academic integrity and fair grading, and more. Written for instructors who have little to no experience designing and teaching online courses or who are teaching online courses developed in a hurry, this is an approachable, efficient guide to the real problems of everyday distance education.

Daniel Hillman is Associate Director of Instructional Design in the Office of Distance Education at Metropolitan College of Boston University, USA.

Robert Schudy is Associate Professor Emeritus of Computer Science at Metropolitan College of Boston University, USA.

Anatoly Temkin is Chair of the Computer Science Department at Metropolitan College of Boston University, USA.

Winning Online Instruction

A Q&A for Higher Education Faculty

Daniel Hillman
Robert Schudy
Anatoly Temkin

NEW YORK AND LONDON

Cover image: Getty Images

First published 2022
by Routledge
605 Third Avenue, New York, NY 10158

and by Routledge
4 Park Square, Milton Park, Abingdon, Oxon, OX14 4RN

Routledge is an imprint of the Taylor & Francis Group, an informa business

© 2022 Daniel Hillman, Robert Schudy, and Anatoly Temkin

The right of Daniel Hillman, Robert Schudy, and Anatoly Temkin to be identified as authors of this work has been asserted in accordance with sections 77 and 78 of the Copyright, Designs and Patents Act 1988.

All rights reserved. No part of this book may be reprinted or reproduced or utilised in any form or by any electronic, mechanical, or other means, now known or hereafter invented, including photocopying and recording, or in any information storage or retrieval system, without permission in writing from the publishers.

Trademark notice: Product or corporate names may be trademarks or registered trademarks, and are used only for identification and explanation without intent to infringe.

Library of Congress Cataloging-in-Publication Data
A catalog record for this title has been requested

ISBN: 978-0-367-74770-1 (hbk)
ISBN: 978-0-367-75165-4 (pbk)
ISBN: 978-1-00-316128-8 (ebk)

DOI: 10.4324/9781003161288

Typeset in Bembo
by Newgen Publishing UK

This book is dedicated to all faculty who were pushed into teaching online during the pandemic and have been courageously doing their best.

Contents

Acknowledgments xiii
List of figure and tables xiv
Preface: Online education in the age of the pandemic xvi
About this book xviii

1 The basics of teaching online 1
   1.1 How do I make my online teaching as effective as my on-campus teaching? 1
   1.2 What are the different types of online instruction? 2
   1.3 How can my synchronous and asynchronous content complement each other? 3
   1.4 How long will it take me to learn to teach online? 4
   1.5 Does teaching online courses take more work than on-campus courses? 5
   1.6 Why can't I just put a video of my on-campus class lecture online? 5
   References 6

2 Developing online teaching skills 8
   2.1 What skills do I need to begin online teaching? 8
   2.2 How can I avoid looking like a novice when I first teach online? 9
   2.3 How do I become more effective teaching with online tools? 10
   2.4 How can asking questions help my online teaching? 11
   2.5 Can I interact online in the same ways I do on campus? 12
   2.6 What changes do I need to make to my lectures for online? 12
   2.7 How do I adjust my lecture material to fit into the available time? 14
   2.8 How do I use my familiar classroom teaching methods online? 14
   2.9 Can I teach subjects that require labs online, like sciences, nursing or physical therapy? 16
   References 18

3 What happens in a typical week online   19
   3.1 What should I have in my online course? 19
   3.2 What's teaching like in an online classroom? 20
   3.3 What's a typical week like in an online course? 22
   3.4 How many students might I have in an online course? 23
   3.5 How do I make my teaching style clear to students? 24
   3.6 How should I dress when teaching online? 25
   3.7 How can I make my personality come through in online courses? 26
   References 26

4 Getting more comfortable using online teaching tools   28
   4.1 How do I set up my workspace for teaching online? 28
   4.2 How should I set up my camera, lighting, and background? 29
   4.3 What technology do I need to learn to teach online successfully? 30
   4.4 What do I need to know to use my learning management system? 31
   4.5 What do I need to know to use my videoconferencing system? 32
   4.6 Should I use my classroom slides online? 34
   Reference 36

5 Designing online courses   37
   5.1 Should I use a publisher's online course, develop my own, or a combination? 37
   5.2 How do I get started developing an online course? 37
   5.3 How do I create a course map? 38
   5.4 How should I order the learning activities? 41
   5.5 How do I want to have discussions in my online course? 42
   5.6 What's a course development plan and how do I create one? 42
   5.7 What's a course template and how will it help me and my students? 44
   5.8 How do I figure out which technologies will best support my learning activities? 45
   5.9 How do I decide whether or not to adopt a technology for my course? 46
   5.10 How can designing for accessibility make my course better? 47
   References 48

6 Developing asynchronous elements of online courses   49
   6.1 What's a study guide and how do I create one? 49
   6.2 Why should I make videos for my course? 50
   6.3 How do I make videos for my course? 51
   6.4 Should I use augmented reality and virtual reality when teaching online? 53
   6.5 How can I use collaboration tools to improve communication? 54
   6.6 How can I develop my online course to include student projects and presentations? 55

6.7 How can I develop an online course in a hurry? Can't I just record my regular lecture? 57
  6.8 How can instructional designers and other staff help me? 58
  6.9 How can I work most effectively with instructional designers? 58
  References 59

7 Developing and teaching blended courses 61
  7.1 What's a blended course? 61
  7.2 How do I use my online course materials in a "flipped" course? 62
  7.3 What's different about teaching a blended course? 63
  7.4 How much effort does it take to prepare and teach a blended course? 64
  7.5 How do I transition my on-campus course to blended? 65
  7.6 How do I use a blended course to develop a fully online course? 68
  7.7 How do I teach with some of my students on-campus and some online? 68
  7.8 How do I encourage communications between on-campus and online students? 69
  References 70

8 Teaching online courses 72
  8.1 How long should my synchronous lectures be? 72
  8.2 How do I schedule synchronous lectures for my online course? 73
  8.3 How many hours will I need to spend on synchronous instruction each week? 73
  8.4 How and when do I do discussions online? 74
  8.5 When should faculty participate in online discussions? 75
  8.6 How do I perform assignment reviews and solution walkthroughs? 76
  8.7 How do I make assignments more interactive for online students? 77
  8.8 How do I know if my online course content is interactive and engaging? 79
  8.9 How do I fix non-technical problems in my online course? 81
  8.10 How much should I communicate with my students when I'm teaching online? 82
  8.11 How do I manage online "office hours"? 83
  8.12 How should I provide feedback to my online students? 84
  8.13 What should be the tone of my email with my students? 85
  8.14 What are the benefits of communicating with online students before and after courses run? 86
  8.15 What are some of the practical advantages for faculty of teaching online? 87
  8.16 What are some of the practical challenges for faculty who teach online? 88
  8.17 Will teaching online advance my career as faculty? 89
  References 89

9 Working with teaching assistants and other faculty 91
9.1 *How can TAs help me and my online students? 91*
9.2 *How do I select, train, mentor, and support my online TAs? 92*
9.3 *How do I manage the workload distribution across my online TAs? 93*
9.4 *How do I ensure that my online TAs are grading consistently? 94*
9.5 *How can I co-teach an online course with other faculty? 94*
9.6 *How do I bring in guest lecturers to speak to my online class? 95*
References 96

10 Addressing online student issues 97
10.1 *How do I help students make the transition to online? 97*
10.2 *How can students engage with their faculty online? 99*
10.3 *Is it important for my online students to discuss what they are studying with each other? 99*
10.4 *How do I set online student expectations on grading? 100*
10.5 *How many hours per week are online students expected to study? 100*
10.6 *How do I know if my online students are attending class? 101*
10.7 *How do I encourage my online students to participate in synchronous sessions? 102*
10.8 *How do I interact with online students in synchronous sessions? 102*
10.9 *How do I help my online students work in groups? 103*
10.10 *How can my online students work on group projects? 104*
10.11 *How can my students do presentations online? 105*
References 105

11 Working with online students who may need extra help 107
11.1 *How do I let my online students know that I am available to help them succeed in the course? 107*
11.2 *How do I motivate my online students to study and learn? 108*
11.3 *How do I get my online students interested in learning what I am teaching? 109*
11.4 *How can I help my online students feel more connected and less isolated? 110*
11.5 *Are there any special considerations when teaching adult students online? 111*
11.6 *How can I help online students who need prerequisite or advanced material? 112*
11.7 *How do I identify struggling online students? 114*
11.8 *How do I help struggling online students? 115*
11.9 *How do I handle overly assertive or aggressive online students? 117*
11.10 *How do I handle online student misconduct? 117*
References 118

12 Getting help for online students with nonacademic issues   120
    12.1 How do I get help for my online students on nonacademic issues? *120*
    12.2 How do I get help for online students with emotional or behavioral challenges? *121*
    12.3 How can I help my online students who are not fluent in the language of instruction? *121*
    12.4 How can I help less-privileged students succeed online? *122*
    12.5 How can I accommodate online students from significantly different time zones, countries, and cultures? *123*
    12.6 How can I accommodate online students with disabilities? *124*
    References *125*

13 Resolving technical problems in online courses   126
    13.1 How can online faculty and students get technical support? *126*
    13.2 How do I troubleshoot online technical issues? *127*
    13.3 How can I prevent audio problems such as feedback and noise? *128*
    13.4 What do I do when a student can't see something in my online course? *129*

14 Promoting academic integrity in online courses   131
    14.1 What's the best way to use a grade book for online students? *131*
    14.2 How can I reward online students for insightful participation? *133*
    14.3 How do I provide feedback when grading online student submissions? *134*
    14.4 How do I teach my online students about academic integrity? *134*
    14.5 How do I review assignment solutions with students online and still ensure academic integrity? *135*
    14.6 How can I ensure that online students are doing their own assignments and projects? *136*
    14.7 How do I make it harder for my students to cheat on online tests? *138*
    14.8 How can exams be proctored online, and what are the tradeoffs? *140*
    14.9 How do I encourage online students to turn on their webcams? *143*
    References *144*

15 Making online courses better   146
    15.1 How can I teach my online course better next time? *146*
    15.2 How can I use student feedback and evaluations to improve my online course? *147*
    15.3 How do I determine if my online course meets its learning objectives? *149*
    15.4 How do I know if my online course needs to be updated? *150*

15.5 How can I work with other faculty to improve my online courses? 152
15.6 How can I make my online course fit better into the program? 153
References 154

Appendices	155
Appendix A: Creating asynchronous lectures	*156*
Appendix B: Integrating prerequisite review material—Module 0	*162*
Appendix C: Conducting synchronous sessions	*164*
Appendix D: Creating and supervising asynchronous online discussions	*168*
Appendix E: Creating formative evaluations for asynchronous lectures	*171*
Appendix F: Creating and updating tests in your LMS	*174*
Appendix G: Creating grading rubrics	*180*
Appendix H: Managing audio for synchronous sessions	*188*
Appendix I: Dealing with technology problems during class	*190*
Glossary	192

Acknowledgments

We wish to thank the following people:

Claudia HCQ Sorsby, for her comprehensive and thoughtful reviews of all drafts of this book, and for pointing out instances where our writing caused semantic angst.

Dan Schwartz at Routledge for guiding us through the editorial process. Again.

Those who provided us with thoughtful suggestions and comments: Adam Arakelian, Elena Garofoli, Alyssa Kariofyllis, Warren Mansur, Jack Polnar, Erin Salius, Fawn Thompson, and Dawson Williams.

Figure and tables

Figure

A.1　Basic structure of an asynchronous course　157

Tables

1.1	Touch in synchronous and asynchronous courses	2
1.2	Comparison of effort for teaching tasks performed on-campus and online	6
2.1	Classroom interactions and their corresponding online counterparts	13
2.2	Common classroom teaching methods and how to use them online	15
4.1	Activities and tools needed for online teaching	30
5.1	Possible content of a module map	39
5.2	Sequence of module learning activities	41
5.3	Discussion goals and how to support them	42
5.4	Part of a simple course development plan	43
6.1	A typical module study guide	50
6.2	Common type of collaboration tools and how they improve communication	55
7.1	Common blended formats	62
7.2	On-campus learning activities and how to adapt them for a blended course	66
8.1	Common situations and faculty responses	85
11.1	Common problem areas for struggling students and what we recommend	116
12.1	Problems faced by less-privileged students and how to help them	123
13.1	Troubleshooting an item that isn't rendering on a web page	129
14.1	Question sets	138
14.2	Student tests created from question sets	139

14.3	Searchable questions and mechanisms for creating their unsearchable counterparts	140
C.1	Common types of synchronous sessions and how to run them	165
F.1	Mean score ranges and what to do in each case	177
F.2	Discriminant ranges and what to do in each case	178
F.3	Common errors in test setup and ways to correct them	179
G.1	Assignment grading rubric	181
G.2	Example of a discussion grading rubric for an introductory course	184
G.3	Example of an asynchronous class-participation rubric	185
I.1	Common technical problems and what you can do about them	190

Preface: Online education in the age of the pandemic

We wrote this book so that faculty in higher education can quickly find answers to their questions about online education. We assume throughout that you already know how to teach, and just want to know how best to translate your knowledge to effective teaching online (Nilson & Goodson, 2018).

Traditional books about distance education describe its theory, history, and various strategies for teaching online (Moore & Kearsley, 2012; Moore, 2013). Their general theses are that online education has great potential, particularly with asynchronous content, and someday it will revolutionize learning (Simpson, 2006). Although there was huge progress over the last two decades, it was still considered subordinate to traditional, on-campus teaching (Chen, 2009; Elnikova et al., 2020).

Then, in 2020, the COVID-19 pandemic closed on-campus teaching across the world. Online education went mainstream almost overnight, as nearly all faculty were required to teach online, with no preparation, no training, and little support. They did the best they could under the circumstances, but the desperate rush gave many faculty and students a poor introduction to distance education (Sari & Nayir, 2020).

Those of us with many years of distance education experience know that developing online programs requires time, preparation, and expertise. At institutions with longstanding online programs, administrators took pains to label this frantic improvisation *remote learning* to differentiate it from *online learning* (Williamson, Eynon, & Potter, 2020).

Whatever it's called, many institutions have seen the ways that even rushed, thrown-together online learning can help all their students learn, even when on-campus education has returned to normal. For example, the immediate feedback of online practice tests helps students both online and on campus, especially those who are struggling. It also helps faculty, by reducing the amount of time they need to spend answering student questions.

So online learning, in one form or another, is here to stay. Recognizing this, many faculty want to get more out of it, both for their students and for themselves.

We designed this book to help faculty teach online; it's a reference where you can quickly find what you need. We wrote it in a question-and-answer format to help you quickly get answers to questions you may have, and we ordered the questions so that it also works well if you read it from beginning to end. The questions are grouped into chapters so that if you want to know more about a topic, you can read the whole chapter on it. Topics that are referenced multiple times across the book, such as formative evaluations and rubrics, have their own appendices at the end, where we cover them in more detail. We've also included references throughout, if you want to learn more.

We hope that reading this book will help speed your development as a great online teacher.

About this book

This book has 15 chapters, which progress from the fundamentals of teaching online to more advanced topics, such as using online courses on campus and improving them. Chapters 1 through 4 answer questions about the basics of online teaching for new faculty, and serve as a foundation for the material to come:

> **Chapter 1 – The basics of teaching online** introduces synchronous and asynchronous teaching methods and their respective advantages and challenges.
> **Chapter 2 – Developing online teaching skills** describes online tools, interacting with students, and adapting familiar on-campus teaching methods to online.
> **Chapter 3 – What happens in a typical week online** deals with common learning activities and how they're organized.
> **Chapter 4 – Getting more comfortable using online teaching tools** addresses the use of webcams, microphones, and videoconferencing systems.

Chapters 5 and 6 answer questions about designing and developing online courses:

> **Chapter 5 – Designing online courses** covers the critical planning and course design activities that faculty should complete before they begin building online courses.
> **Chapter 6 – Developing asynchronous elements of online courses** addresses study guides, videos, collaboration tools, and working with instructional designers.

Chapters 7 and 8 answer questions about teaching and using online course material, both online and on campus:

Chapter 7 – Developing and teaching blended courses describes how blended courses are different from purely on-campus or online courses, and how they can be a stepping-stone in developing purely online courses.

Chapter 8 – Teaching online courses describes what you need to do when your online course is running.

Chapters 9 through 12 answer questions about working online with teaching assistants, other faculty, and students:

Chapter 9 – Working with teaching assistants and other faculty addresses how to supervise assistants and assure that they grade fairly, and how to co-teach with colleagues.

Chapter 10 – Addressing online student issues describes ways in which faculty can interact with their online students, give them feedback, and foster student participation and confidence.

Chapter 11 – Working with students who may need extra help covers techniques to motivate, encourage, and guide students who are falling behind or getting ahead, and how faculty can help them succeed.

Chapter 12 – Getting help for students with nonacademic issues deals with how faculty can build and teach courses to accommodate students with disabilities and cultural, economic, and language differences.

Chapters 13 and 14 answer questions about how to resolve technical problems and how to use technology to promote academic integrity:

Chapter 13 – Resolving technical problems in online courses provides solutions for common technical problems.

Chapter 14 – How do I promote academic integrity in online courses offers methods for making cheating more difficult, detecting it, and proctoring tests online.

Finally, Chapter 15 answers questions about how to use what you learned from teaching your courses to improve them and your teaching:

Chapter 15 – Making online courses better deals with how to evaluate online courses and identify ways to make them better.

We have also included a glossary to make the book easier to use. First instances of terms listed in the glossary are presented in **boldface** in each chapter or appendix.

References

Chen, B. (2009). Barriers to adoption of technology mediated distance education in higher-education institutions. *Quarterly Review of Distance Education, 10*(4), 333–338.

Elnikova, G. A., Nikulina, N. N., Gordienko, I. V., & Davityan, M. G. (2020). Distance education in universities: Lessons from the pandemic. *European Journal of Molecular & Clinical Medicine, 7*(1), 3253–3529.

Moore, M. G., & Kearsley, G. (2012). *Distance education: A systems view of online learning* (3rd. ed.). Cengage Learning.

Moore, M. G. (2013). *Handbook of distance education* (3rd. ed.). New York: Routledge.

Nilson, L. B., & Goodson, L. A. (2018). *Online teaching at its best: Merging instructional design with teaching and learning research.* John Wiley & Sons.

Sari, T., & Nayir, F. (2020). Challenges in distance education during the (Covid-19) pandemic period. *Qualitative Research in Education, 9*(3), 328–360.

Simpson, R. L. (2006). See the future of distance education. *Nursing Management, 37*(2), 42–51.

Williamson, B., Eynon, R., & Potter, J. (2020). Pandemic politics, pedagogies and practices: digital technologies and distance education during the coronavirus emergency. *Learning, Media and Technology, 45*(2), 107–114.

Chapter 1

The basics of teaching online

In this chapter we answer basic questions about the different ways of teaching online. We describe **synchronous** and **asynchronous** teaching methods and their respective advantages and challenges. We discuss how to teach online effectively, and how well-developed and well-taught online courses can be even better than on-campus courses.

1.1 How do I make my online teaching as effective as my on-campus teaching?

The effectiveness of online education depends on the skill of the faculty who develop and teach the courses (Wolf, 2006). If you're an effective teacher on campus, you already know most of what you need to know to be an effective teacher online (Clinefelter, 2012). All that you need to do is learn how to use technology to do online what you do in the classroom.

A well-developed online course can be even more effective than an on-campus course, because it can provide more ways for students to learn. Good teaching, regardless of how it's delivered, will provide:

- content in the most logical ways to help students understand it;
- many opportunities for students to test their knowledge and apply it;
- rapid feedback to help students confirm their knowledge and guide them to understand the material;
- extensive student **engagement** with the subject matter, using what they've learned, and solving problems;
- learning and testing that reflects how things are done in practice, when appropriate;
- opportunities for students to interact with their faculty and ask questions; and
- opportunities for students to interact with other students.

DOI: 10.4324/9781003161288-1

1.2 What are the different types of online instruction?

There are basically two kinds of online instruction—synchronous, in which students and faculty interact in real time, and asynchronous, in which students interact with material prepared in advance. Today most synchronous instruction takes place using **videoconferencing** tools, like Zoom or Teams, and most asynchronous instruction takes place using web-based **learning management systems** (**LMS**s), like Blackboard or Canvas. Anything that can be on a website can be included in web-based teaching—text, images, videos, animations, and **interactive objects** (Wimer, 2016).

Teaching well online generally means using both synchronous and asynchronous components. Most classroom teaching methods can be implemented online, with appropriate technology. Some online technologies, such as automatically graded tests implemented in the LMS, will help your students learn and save you time and effort once you've set them up. Similarly, asynchronous online lectures can be very effective; they can pay off with reduced teaching time and less need for synchronous lectures, but they require substantial development effort.

Both synchronous and asynchronous online instruction can vary in the amount of student participation (Davidson-Shivers et al., 2001). Types of instruction may differ primarily by the amount of "**touch**," or interaction, with the course material, the faculty, and other students (Jung et al., 2002). The more a course is like reading a book or watching a movie, the lower the touch. The more a course includes students participating in lively and engaging discussions and interactions with each other and faculty, the higher touch it is. Table 1.1 compares touch in typical synchronous and asynchronous courses.

Table 1.1 Touch in synchronous and asynchronous courses

	Synchronous	Asynchronous
High touch	Videoconferencing meetings between faculty and students, with extensive student-faculty dialogue. These courses often include dialogue between students, sometimes supervised by faculty.	Text- or video-based discussion boards allow students to ask questions, do presentations, and interact with each other and faculty.
Low touch	Webinar presentations where faculty are lecturing and the only way that students can interact is by posting questions in a chat window.	Courses with little or no student-faculty interaction: These include training videos, online tutorials, or massive open online courses (**MOOC**s).

Asynchronous instruction lets you take advantage of many more technologies and teaching options than synchronous instruction. For example, in a synchronous session you have to teach all your students the same material at the same time, while asynchronously some students can spend more time studying what they need, while others may safely skip some material (for more on creating asynchronous lectures, see Appendix A). Another great advantage of asynchronous teaching is that you can explain the same topic in several ways, such as describing it in text, illustrating it with a diagram, or demonstrating it with a video, and your students will be able to use the formats that work best for them.

Online instruction can also be combined with on-campus instruction in a **blended** or **hybrid** course. Blended courses have many advantages, including being easier for first-time online instructors to teach and being more forgiving of rookie mistakes. (For more on blended courses, see Chapter 7.) One of the most important and common types of blended courses are **flipped** courses, in which the students study asynchronous material online and then come to the classroom to discuss the material and do exercises, such as labs.

1.3 How can my synchronous and asynchronous content complement each other?

The most successful courses have both synchronous and asynchronous components, which allow faculty to take advantage of the best qualities of each of these modes of instruction (Olson & McCracken, 2015). An example would be a fully asynchronous course that includes synchronous sessions with faculty for questions and discussion. Everything that you would cover in a synchronous course should be covered in an asynchronous course (Hrastinski, 2008). Our experience has been that faculty prefer to cover increasing amounts of the course content in the asynchronous portions of the courses, until sometimes a textbook may no longer be needed.

Nowadays synchronous content is presented using videoconferencing and asynchronous content is presented as a website, which may contain text, images, and videos, plus more advanced teaching technologies, such as interactive objects. Your students will study your asynchronous content to learn the material, and they'll inevitably have questions about the content and how it applies. Your synchronous sessions should give your students an opportunity to ask those questions and discuss the material with you. If you think that your students may need motivation to study, you may wish to introduce your asynchronous content in a synchronous session to tell your students why it's important.

> Hint: Responding to students' questions synchronously is usually more efficient than asynchronously, so regularly scheduled question-and-answer sessions will help you save time.

1.4 How long will it take me to learn to teach online?

During the first, crisis phase of the pandemic, many faculty got some experience teaching online—whether they wanted it or not—with no time to prepare. Successful online teaching generally requires a great deal of organization and preparation, which added to the difficulties of the situation. You may be tired of Zoom (or FaceTime, Teams, or whatever videoconferencing tools you used then), but you can build on the experience you developed with it, and approach online teaching in a more systematic way.

If you're accustomed to preparing lesson plans and slides in advance, you'll find the transition to online much easier than if you're used to winging it and making up lectures as you go (Cole & Kritzer, 2009). You don't have to learn everything at once, so make it a goal to learn one new thing a semester and integrate it into your courses (Darby & Lang, 2019).

If you're already good at communicating with technology, such as email, chat, and videoconferencing tools, you'll probably learn to teach online quickly (Petrina, 2007). For example, if you're skilled at writing emails and other long-form texts, you'll be able to communicate well with your students using course email, internal messages, and announcements. If you've got experience writing SMS messages, you already know how to text with your students. If you're good at taking pictures and making cat videos, you can use those skills for your courses. If you're comfortable with using social media and sharing those cat videos, you'll probably learn how to use basic LMS functions quickly.

The best way to learn how to teach well quickly is to observe skilled online faculty at work. One of the advantages of online education is that faculty can observe a course without disrupting it, even after it has run. Ideally, faculty who are new to online can be enrolled in a class that they'll teach, to observe those more experienced online instructors.

Having faculty skilled in online teaching as mentors will also accelerate your learning (Lock et al., 2016). Mentors should be enrolled in your courses to observe how you teach and the situations that you're addressing. There is much to learn about online teaching, so you should expect to improve your skills for years, as you gradually become an outstanding online instructor.

1.5 Does teaching online courses take more work than on-campus courses?

Once you're comfortable with the technology, developing and teaching synchronous course components is no more work online than in the classroom (Van de Vord & Pogue, 2012). Developing asynchronous course components does take significantly more effort, but once they've been created, they can reduce teaching effort and improve student outcomes (Spector, 2005).

During the pandemic, when faculty were unable to meet with their students on campus, many adapted in mid-semester, switching on the fly to teaching their courses entirely synchronously online. One advantage of synchronous lecturing is that faculty's existing teaching skills transferred readily to this format, and they were able to continue teaching largely as if they were in the classroom. Another is that synchronous content requires almost no preparation except slides, which most faculty already use in their on-campus courses.

Under more normal circumstances, teaching strong online courses means having a combination of synchronous and asynchronous content, and all the asynchronous components—lectures, videos, quizzes, assignments, and discussions—need to be developed before the course runs.

Basically, creating good asynchronous content is like building a website, which can be a lot of work (Winer, 2016).

All that work pays off, though. Once the course is built, asynchronous content requires virtually no faculty involvement when the course is running, leaving them free to spend more time with the students, answering questions and supervising discussions. LMSs can also speed up grading.

And, when the course is taught again, it's easy to reuse and improve asynchronous material from previous terms—create it once and build on it. Table 1.2 compares the effort between teaching online and on campus, for typical teaching tasks.

1.6 Why can't I just put a video of my on-campus class lecture online?

Unless your lectures are riveting prose and you're a skilled storyteller, your students won't appreciate your reading a lecture to them like an hour-long bedtime story. Good classroom teachers frequently ask their students questions, solicit discussion, and tailor their lecture on the fly to what their students understand and where they need more instruction. You can do the same online in synchronous lectures, where you and your students ask each other questions and discuss the material.

If you've prepared an on-campus lecture and don't have time to develop an asynchronous one, you can deliver it synchronously, as long as you engage

Table 1.2 Comparison of effort for teaching tasks performed on-campus and online

Teaching Task	Comparison of on-campus and online effort
Develop lecture materials	Significantly more effort online, because online lectures need to be written and students expect the writing quality to be comparable to textbooks.
Deliver lecture materials	Once asynchronous lecture materials have been developed, there's minimal effort to deliver them online, whereas faculty must deliver synchronous lectures in full every time.
Develop assignments	Similar low effort, because the same assignments can be used online as on campus.
Grade assignments	About the same amount of effort, unless some of the online grading can be automated.
Develop tests	It takes the same amount of effort to create the content of a test, regardless of how it's delivered. LMSs can help faculty format and randomize questions and answers online. Faculty can also include feedback, which initially increases the effort to create tests, but can be more extensive than what you would write on individual paper tests.
Administer tests	Significantly less effort online, with no need to print paper tests, hand them out, and collect them. Randomization can reduce the need to proctor tests.
Grade tests	If automatically graded tests can be created, grading takes almost no effort online. If online tests include comprehensive feedback, there should be very few student questions.
Grade the course	Easier online, because the LMS adds student grades to the grade book and does the calculations.

your students in dialogue throughout. This allows you to adapt your lecture to your students, as you would in the classroom, and it allows your students to ask you questions.

References

Clinefelter, D. (2012). Best practices in online faculty development. *Learning House Whitepaper* Retrieved January 27, 2021, from www.learninghouse.com/wp-content/uploads/2017/09/Best-Practices-for-Online-Faculty-Development_Web_Final.pdf.

Cole, J. E., & Kritzer, J. B. (2009). Strategies for success: Teaching an online course. *Rural Special Education Quarterly, 28*(4), 36–40.

Darby, F., & Lang, J. M. (2019). *Small teaching online: Applying learning science in online classes.* John Wiley & Sons.

Davidson-Shivers, G.V., Muilenburg, L.Y., & Tanner, E. J. (2001). How do students participate in synchronous and asynchronous online discussions? *Journal of Educational Computing Research, 25*(4), 351–366.

Hrastinski, S. (2008). Asynchronous and synchronous e-learning. *Educause Quarterly, 31*(4), 51–55.

Jung, I., Choi, S., Lim, C., & Leem, J. (2002). Effects of different types of interaction on learning achievement, satisfaction and participation in web-based instruction. *Innovations in Education and Teaching International, 39*(2), 153–162.

Lock, J., Clancy, T., Lisella, R., Rosenau, P., Ferreira, C., & Rainsbury, J. (2016). The lived experiences of instructors co-teaching in higher education. *Brock Education Journal, 26*(1), 22–35.

Olson, J. S., & McCracken, F. E. (2015). Is it worth the effort? The impact of incorporating synchronous lectures into an online course. *Online Learning, 19*(2), 1–12.

Petrina, S. (2007). *Advanced teaching methods for the technology classroom*. Hershey, PA: Information Science Publishing.

Spector, J. M. (2005). Time demands in online instruction. *Distance Education, 26*(1), 5–27.

Van de Vord, R., & Pogue, K. (2012). Teaching time investment: Does online really take more time than face-to-face? *International Review of Research in Open and Distributed Learning, 13*(3), 132–146.

Wimer, K. (2016). Designing asynchronous content. In A. Hicks (Ed.), *Got a minute? Instruction tune-up for time pressed librarians*. Denver, CO: University of Denver.

Wolf, P. D. (2006). Best practices in the training of faculty to teach online. *Journal of Computing in Higher Education, 17*(2), 47–78.

Chapter 2

Developing online teaching skills

In this chapter we describe how faculty can begin to learn how to teach online, including using online tools, interacting with their students, adapting their on-campus lecture style and familiar on-campus teaching methods to online, encouraging questions and dialogue, and the ever popular, "How do I avoid looking like a novice when I first teach online?"

2.1 What skills do I need to begin online teaching?

First, just recognize that the process of teaching is fundamentally the same, regardless of how you do it. Faculty present some material, then ask students a question, and then faculty respond to the answer by continuing or by explaining the material in a different way (Sinclair & Coulthard, 1975; Mehan, 1978). This is the most common kind of **synchronous** teaching, and it can also be done **asynchronously** with **formative evaluations**. (For more on formative evaluations, see Appendix E.) Most of what you do in the classroom is the same online; all that differs is the technology that makes it possible online.

Second, you'll need to learn how to do the most common operations in the course **LMS**, including how to send your students emails using the course email system, how to grade submissions, and how to use the grade book (Black et al., 2007). If you don't have someone to upload, link, configure, and test content in the LMS, you'll also need to learn how to do those tasks yourself. Your institution may have training and support for faculty in how to use the LMS. If not, the vendors of LMSs also offer training on their websites.

Third, you'll need to learn how to use your program's **videoconferencing** system. Some of the recent systems, like Zoom, are easy to use, and you probably already have experience with them. You'll need to learn to host sessions, including sharing your screen and muting people's mics. You should record yourself practicing these things, and you should watch your

DOI: 10.4324/9781003161288-2

recordings to get better. (If your audio quality isn't as good as you'd like, see Appendix H. If you don't look as good as you'd like, see Chapter 6.)

Fourth, one of the best ways to learn how to teach well online is to attend an experienced online faculty's course or watch videos of someone teaching online (Lock et al., 2016). You can learn the nuts and bolts of teaching online from faculty training, provided by your institution or your LMS vendor. You'll learn subtleties, such as course dynamics and how to respond to students, from experienced faculty (McKenzie et al., 2006).

Fifth, when you're teaching online, you'll occasionally encounter technical problems that interfere with your ability to communicate with your students. The most common problems are audio and network issues. When you or your students have technical issues, you'll need to know how to contact technical support, and you should also learn how to use alternative technologies if one fails (see Chapter 13).

2.2 How can I avoid looking like a novice when I first teach online?

Many faculty who are new to online teaching have the same nightmare—they're teaching a big class with lots of students, and all of a sudden, things stop working, and no matter what they do, nothing helps. Students call out contradicting advice. They start to talk among themselves, chaos descends… then the faculty wake up in a cold sweat.

The most basic preparation for teaching online is accepting that things will go wrong, and that it'll be okay. There are many ways of accomplishing teaching objectives online; if one doesn't work, be ready to try others. For example, if the LMS is down, you can probably email your students an extract of the lecture. If the LMS or course videoconferencing system is down, you can probably meet with them at a collaboration site, such as Google Groups. If a video lecture doesn't work, try using audio and posting the slides where students can see them, or again, move to a collaboration site.

> Hint: Be sure that all of your slides have numbers on them for reference. It's much easier to say "slide eight" than "the slide with the yellow table that starts with…".

The most difficult technical problem to deal with is if your internet connection fails; in these situations, you can tether your smartphone to your computer as a backup internet connection (if this fails, use your phone to let your students know of the outage, if at all possible). You may even be able to conduct synchronous lectures using said smartphone. One of the authors has taught part of a course while visiting an island in Maine that had neither power nor internet, by tethering his computer to his smartphone, and powering the whole thing with a car battery at the end of a dock, where he had the best cell signal. Students appreciated both the resourcefulness of the faculty and the background view of the water.

The other basic preparation is to practice using the tools without your students being present. For example, you can practice displaying and changing slides and sharing the screen on your own, maybe asking family or friends to stand in for the students. Even if you don't have a chance to practice beforehand, you'll find that the second time you give an online lecture it'll go much more smoothly and you'll be more relaxed (Ulmer et al., 2007).

> Hint: It's helpful to record your practice sessions and review them. You're sure to notice ways to improve your presentation.

2.3 How do I become more effective teaching with online tools?

It's normal that people feel uncomfortable with technology when they're new to using it (Prensky, 2007). Having an audience when you're learning something new may make the experience scarier. Nobody wants their students to see that they don't know how to use tools in the most effective way. You can do several things to help yourself become more proficient with online tools, such as watching video tutorials and practicing what you'll do in your online classes.

It helps a great deal to practice using any new tool, doing what you plan to do in class. You can also practice with another person, who may provide feedback and guidance. They don't even have to be in the same room with you if you use a videoconferencing tool. You can also take an online course to see how your colleagues work—just be sure that the course is taught the same way that you'll be teaching (Darby & Lang, 2019).

Many faculty gain skill and confidence quickly from watching online videos of people using teaching tools. These online videos typically cover only the basic operations; if you want to learn the less obvious parts of the software, so that you'll look like a guru to your students, read the documentation. If your institution or the software vendor has webinars for faculty, these can also be very helpful. Some institutions have IT staff or **instructional designers** who are experienced with the tools and available to answer faculty questions.

> Hint: The best way to feel comfortable with tools is to learn more about them than you need to perform your job.

It also helps improve faculty confidence if they have someone online with them in the course who is skilled in using the tools. Some programs have staff or teaching assistants (TAs) who can do this. Most faculty need this help and reassurance for only a short while, while they're learning new tools, so it doesn't have be expensive. When you're learning a new online tool, let your students know that you're still in the process of learning it. If you manage your students' expectations, they'll accept this and may even try to help you.

2.4 How can asking questions help my online teaching?

If your on-campus teaching style involves asking your students many questions throughout each lecture, you'll find that transfers well to online. If you tend to lecture for long stretches on campus without asking or answering students' questions, you'll find that this won't work well online, because your students will feel more isolated from you without face-to-face contact. Fortunately, online teaching provides many simple approaches for asking and answering questions.

In synchronous lectures, you can and should ask questions often. If this doesn't come naturally to you, here are some tricks to get you in the habit:

- Put questions on the slides along with the content as you build them, if there's room.
- Insert slides of questions between your content slides.
- Set a timer on your phone or watch as a reminder to ask questions, every few minutes.
- Ask your students if they have any questions when you finish each slide or topic.

It helps to teach a course synchronously—either on-campus or online—before developing an asynchronous version, because you'll get a sense of where students tend to need additional instruction. For example, one of the authors had taught an on-campus course in calculus often enough to know that students were frequently confused by the concept of the chain rule. So, when setting up the online version of that course, at that point he created several types of additional instruction—examples, explanations, and self-check quizzes—that were available to the students online, just by clicking a link.

Asynchronous online teaching also lets you give students immediate feedback, regardless of when they answer the question. Since asynchronous lectures are written out ahead of time, asking questions during them is akin to offering lots of short quizzes or tests for students, with immediate answers that you've had time to think about and polish, instead of being off the cuff.

This sort of feedback can take the form of formative evaluations, which don't count in their grades, or **summative assessments**, which do. In formative evaluations, students test themselves to see if they understand the topics as they learn them. (For more on formative evaluations, see Appendix E.) A good formative evaluation will provide guidance based on the students' answers, addressing whatever their incorrect answers reveal that they need to learn. For example, if the question is, "Does a sentence always need to have a subject and a verb?" and the student answers "yes," then the feedback may include examples of exceptions, such as "Marvelous!"

Summative assessments, which do count toward students' grades, have always featured asynchronous feedback. It'll help your students' learning and satisfaction if you configure them so that the grades are released immediately, so they can learn from the detailed explanations and be better prepared for the rest of the course. To maintain **academic integrity** with immediate release, you should use randomization of questions and answers. (For more on this, see Chapter 14.)

2.5 Can I interact online in the same ways I do on campus?

You can interact with your online students in most of the ways you would in the classroom. Different technologies for various kinds of asynchronous online interaction are provided by LMSs, while most synchronous online interaction uses videoconferencing. Table 2.1 shows classroom interactions and their corresponding asynchronous and synchronous online counterparts.

> Hint: If you want to send physical objects to your students, such as wine samples for a wine-tasting course, you'll need to plan ahead so they can be shipped.

2.6 What changes do I need to make to my lectures for online?

Teaching a synchronous online course is similar to lecturing in the classroom. The main difference is that, because you and your students can't see

Table 2.1 Classroom interactions and their corresponding online counterparts

Classroom interaction	Asynchronous online interaction	Synchronous online interaction
announcements	delivered via the LMS announcement facility	conducted using videoconferencing
lecture	pre-written lectures delivered using the LMS	
recitation	formative evaluation questions with feedback written by faculty; online discussion boards with questions and evaluations posted by faculty	
discussion	online discussion boards in which students and faculty participate	
talking one-on-one	private posts or email in the LMS (often this is better done synchronously)	
office hours	private posts or email in the LMS (better done synchronously)	
email	as used in the classroom, but probably with the LMS's email	chat
distributing and collecting papers and handouts	files delivered and collected using the LMS	there is no corresponding synchronous online interaction

each other very well, it's hard to "read" body language, so you need to make more of an effort to engage, affirm, and reassure them. You'll also need to make more of an effort to ask questions and otherwise determine how well your students understand the material. Be sure to make it clear to your students that you really value their questions and feedback. We recommend that you award class contribution credit for good student questions and answers.

Teaching an asynchronous course is very different from teaching in the classroom. Developing an asynchronous course is more like writing a textbook for your students, with quizzes, review questions, and assignments, and then helping them as they study what you wrote. You'll have to predict when your students will need examples, use multiple ways to assess their understanding, and offer guidance in areas where they need help. For this reason, it's helpful to have taught a course synchronously before developing it for asynchronous delivery. (For more on developing asynchronous content, see Chapter 6. For more on creating asynchronous lectures, see Appendix A.)

2.7 How do I adjust my lecture material to fit into the available time?

Sometimes you have too much material, and other times you need to add material. Experienced faculty continually adjust the content of their courses, adding new material and deleting material that is no longer as important. Faculty can also adjust the length of their lectures during this process. The average person speaks 150 words per minute (Miller et al., 1976), so a typical, 50-minute academic lecture has about 7,500 words in it.

Ideally, your synchronous sessions would be like a **flipped** classroom, where you engage with your students on the subject matter that they've already studied asynchronously (for more on flipped classrooms, see Chapter 7). This isn't always possible, because the asynchronous material may not be complete or pedagogically strong enough, or because your students might not have done the work yet, so you may need to cover some topics in a synchronous lecture format. One good technique is to cover key topics at a summary level that has enough detail to remind students of what they have studied and any questions that they want to ask.

If your online course has significant asynchronous content, your synchronous lectures won't need to cover everything that you would cover on campus. They should cover the topics that you expect your students to struggle with, so they can ask you questions. (For more on creating asynchronous lectures, see Appendix A.)

2.8 How do I use my familiar classroom teaching methods online?

Most classroom teaching methods can be implemented online, and some teaching methods can be implemented online that don't work well in the classroom (Lewis & Abdul-Hamid, 2006). The main limitations of teaching online through videoconferencing are the constraints of the software, cameras, and microphones. They generally make it more difficult to "read" the body language and facial expressions of your students to see if they understand, though, paradoxically, videoconferencing can make it easier to see individual faces in large courses, with several hundred or more students. This assumes students have chosen to turn their cameras on, of course.

Things that you can do easily online that you can't do in most classrooms are recording the sessions for students to review and dividing the class into small groups in **breakout rooms**. Table 2.2 summarizes common classroom methods and how to use them online.

Developing online teaching skills 15

> Hint: Synchronous online activities tend to work better when there are no more than a dozen students, because they have more opportunities to participate.

Table 2.2 Common classroom teaching methods and how to use them online

Classroom method	How to use it online
demonstration	You should embed slides, video, or animations that you would show in a classroom in an LMS, where students can review them as often as they wish.
case study	The asynchronous portion of a case study may be posted in the LMS. Online, the discussion portion can be asynchronous or synchronous. If it's synchronous, we recommend using videoconferencing breakout rooms to keep the groups small enough for discussions.
debate	A small number of people can participate at once. Use videoconferencing breakout rooms to keep the groups small enough for discussions.
discussion	Synchronous discussion with videoconferencing supports only a few active participants at a time, unless you use breakout rooms. Asynchronous discussions allow more students to participate, and more time for thought before answering.
guest lectures	This works better online, because guest lecturers do not have to come to the classroom—or even to campus.
in-class labs	Some labs, such as computer labs, audio labs, or computer simulations, require only students' own computers. Chemistry and many other labs require additional apparatus and materials.
students asking questions during a lecture	The same as in the classroom, within the limitations of videoconferencing.
problem-solving/ brainstorming	This is usually a synchronous activity. If the class is small, this can be done with all students at once using videoconferencing. If the class is large, split students into groups with breakout rooms.
projects	These are usually asynchronous activities, and may be appropriate for small groups. The groups will need ways to communicate and collaborate, such as discussion boards and videoconferencing, and places to share files.
review sessions	Synchronous review sessions are the same as in the classroom, except that they can be recorded. Asynchronous review sessions can be done as practice tests with extensive feedback.

(continued)

Table 2.2 (Cont.)

Classroom method	How to use it online
roleplay, seminars, question sessions	These are usually similar to how they're done in the classroom, except they use videoconferencing and may be recorded.
site visits, field work	If you are planning on presenting a site visit online, you can make a video or do it live. If you have assigned field work to your students, they can go to different places, which can improve the overall coverage and diversity.
student presentations with student and faculty questions	These are done as in the classroom, except that in larger classes presentations may be to students' groups, rather than the whole class.
take-home quizzes/ assignments	These are done as in the classroom, except that quizzes should be implemented, and assignments distributed and submitted, via the LMS.

2.9 Can I teach subjects that require labs online, like sciences, nursing or physical therapy?

The theory of laboratory subjects can be taught online, and procedures can be demonstrated, but teaching hands-on skills online requires that students perform tasks they need to learn (Gazza, 2017). Traditional on-campus programs teach hands-on skills in laboratory classrooms, where students have access to lab apparatus, materials, and safety equipment, and where they are supervised by faculty. Fortunately, most of the learning objectives of lab classes can be met online.

Techniques for teaching labs in online courses depend on the learning objectives and subject matter. The following sections outline teaching methods for common subjects.

Physics lab courses have long included labs in which students gain experience with forces, inertia, levers, and basic electricity and magnetism. Relevant experiments can be performed with simple, inexpensive apparatus that can be included in a lab kit that students purchase or rent, just as they purchase or rent textbooks. A web search will find many physics lab kits. Most are at the elementary or high school level, but some are at the college level. Most cost less than a textbook.

Some advanced physics labs, such as those on digital electronics, are inexpensive, but some may require that students spend a few days in a well-equipped laboratory; for example, cryogenics students cannot be expected to have liquid nitrogen and helium at home. These laboratories may be at the institution offering the online lab course, or at another school or facility near the students.

Chemistry lab courses need to address safety concerns when students do experiments with chemicals. Students need to have apparatus and chemicals for their experiments, both of which involve risk if used improperly. Safety measures developed for on-campus chemistry labs, such as using the smallest feasible quantities of reagents, also apply online. Chemistry lab kits that include labware and chemicals for common basic experiments are available for purchase, for prices comparable to textbooks.

Online students need to have a space for their experiments, and their faculty should verify that the space is appropriate. The space is commonly in the kitchen, so precautions should be taken to prevent food contamination with lab chemicals; faculty can design experiments that do not use toxic substances. However, if the learning objectives include gaining experience with apparatus such as laboratory-quality scales or fume hoods, then students will need to perform experiments at the institution offering the online chemistry lab course, or at another school or laboratory near them.

Nursing, physical therapy, and other medical disciplines also require that students gain experience working with patients, with appropriate supervision and evaluation. Like on-campus programs, online programs need to have relationships with hospitals or other facilities so students can work with patients, and do their practical work supervised by local, appropriately qualified practitioners. The lecture format for online courses that teach hands-on skills should include the theoretical material, and it should also include demonstrations of the hands-on techniques. These can be done with multimedia, including video, videoconferencing, and potentially **virtual reality**.

Music and other sound-centric labs can differ in implementation and difficulty. If a lab only requires that students listen to sounds or produce them individually, this can usually be handled using personal computers, headsets, and conferencing systems. For example, voice and foreign-language lessons can be given effectively via videoconferencing. Group activities can be achieved by recording the students individually, and digitally combining the recordings, though it is technically complex and the experience is not like being together in the same space.

Computer labs can be implemented in online courses in several ways. Students can often run the laboratory software on their own computers; examples include compilers and integrated development environments for computer programming courses and database management systems for database courses. One challenge with this is that the applications need to be available for the type of computers that students have. Virtualization can also be used to create labs that students run on their own computers.

Another challenge is that sometimes it isn't feasible for students to run an application on their own computers, because of the resource requirements or licensing. In these situations, the best approach is usually for the institution to provide students internet access to the applications, hosted at the school or by a third party. This has allowed our students to gain experience with big data databases and public cloud computing. A complementary approach is to use virtualization technology, which allows one computer to act as if it were many; this enables schools to virtualize labs for their students, and have labs only use computer resources when the students are using them. For example, we created a virtual lab for an IT security course that allows students to attack and defend the computer systems of a small enterprise, all virtualized on their own PCs.

References

Black, E. W., Beck, D., Dawson, K., Jinks, S., & DiPietro, M. (2007). The other side of the LMS: Considering implementation and use in the adoption of an LMS in online and blended learning environments. *TechTrends, 51*(2), 35–39.

Darby, F., & Lang, J. M. (2019). *Small teaching online: Applying learning science in online classes*. John Wiley & Sons.

Gazza, E. A. (2017). The experience of teaching online in nursing education. *Journal of Nursing Education, 56*(6), 343–349.

Lewis, C. C., & Abdul-Hamid, H. (2006). Implementing effective online teaching practices: Voices of exemplary faculty. *Innovative Higher Education, 31*(2), 83–98.

Lock, J., Clancy, T., Lisella, R., Rosenau, P., Ferreira, C., & Rainsbury, J. (2016). The lived experiences of instructors co-teaching in higher education. *Brock Education Journal, 26*(1), 22–35.

McKenzie, B. K., Ozkan, B. C., & Layton, K. (2006). Tips for administrators in promoting distance programs using peer mentoring. *Online Journal of Distance Learning Administration, 9*(2), 1–8.

Mehan, H. (1978). Structuring school structure. *Harvard Educational Review, 48*(1), 32–64.

Miller, N., Maruyama, G., Beaber, R. J., & Valone, K. (1976). Speed of speech and persuasion. *Journal of Personality and Social Psychology, 34*(4), 615–624.

Prensky, M. (2007). How to teach with technology: Keeping both teachers and students comfortable in an era of exponential change. *Emerging Technologies for Learning, 2*(4), 40–46.

Sinclair, J. M., & Coulthard, R. M. (1975). *Towards an analysis of discourse*. Oxford: Oxford University Press.

Ulmer, L. W., Watson, L. W., & Derby, D. (2007). Perceptions of higher education faculty members on the value of distance education. *Quarterly Review of Distance Education, 8*(1), 59–70.

Chapter 3

What happens in a typical week online

In this chapter we describe what it's like to teach in a typical week online, including common **learning activities** and how they're organized. We also cover how to convey your teaching style and personality online.

3.1 What should I have in my online course?

The content of your online course will depend on what you're teaching, how you teach it, and the resources you have to develop it. We recommend that you have both **synchronous** and **asynchronous** activities in your course. Your synchronous activities will probably use **videoconferencing** (except for students with slow internet access issues, in which cases you'll most likely provide them with audio, since it takes less **bandwidth**). Your asynchronous activities will probably include tests and discussions, and they may include written lectures with videos and other objects. Asynchronous content takes longer to develop, so you may need to begin with mainly synchronous activities.

> Hint: In our syllabi, we use the term "**module**" instead of "week" to allow more flexibility, as some topics don't fit neatly in a week. This also lets us use the same course for seven- or fourteen-week formats, and the only thing we have to change is the due dates.

Your synchronous sessions should include both course and module introductions. This will give you an opportunity to share your love of the subject matter and your students an opportunity to ask questions about what they'll be studying. We also recommend that you conduct at least one session devoted to your students' questions; it should be near the end of the module, before the assignments and tests are due. We also suggest that you conduct

DOI: 10.4324/9781003161288-3

at least one hour of synchronous teaching near the middle of the module, where you go over the main points. Unfortunately, faculty often don't have enough time to develop all of the material for asynchronous courses, so they must cover some of it synchronously.

The best online courses cover all of the subject matter asynchronously, with opportunities for students to engage with their faculty synchronously. Asynchronous lectures enable powerful teaching methods, such as inline **formative evaluations**, that can make an online course more like one-on-one tutoring. It's also easier to integrate videos, images, animations, and **interactive objects** into asynchronous content than synchronous. (For more on creating asynchronous lectures, see Appendix A.)

You'll need to create at least two kinds of asynchronous **learning objects**—**assessments** and discussions—and you'll want to integrate them into the **LMS**'s grade book. If you've created assignments for your course on campus, it's easy to add them to your online course and connect them to the course calendar and grade book. If you've created tests and exams for your on-campus class, you'll need to learn how to enter the questions into the LMS or have someone do it for you. (For more on creating and updating tests, see Appendix F.)

Students in online courses benefit from asynchronous discussions, in which faculty post seed questions and students post responses (Dennen, 2005). These discussions allow students more time to think before responding, so their posts are of higher quality. The synchronous classroom doesn't support asynchronous posts, so if you haven't taught online before, this may be new to you. (For more on how to create and grade discussion questions, see Chapter 8 and Appendix D.)

The time and other resources that you have to develop your online course will directly affect what's in it. This includes how much time you have to develop course material, whether or not other people with specialized skills will be working with you, and the hardware and software that's available to you. (See Chapters 5 and 6, where we describe how to design and develop your course.)

3.2 What's teaching like in an online classroom?

The way you teach in an online classroom depends on how your course is designed; the biggest difference is between synchronous and asynchronous.

Teaching synchronously online isn't significantly different from a regular, on-campus class. When you teach a synchronous class, you come prepared with your slides and discussion topics, and you might do a lecture, recitation, discussion, or other things you do on campus. You'll just be using videoconferencing and other software to interact with your students, instead of interacting in person. You may even be teaching your online students from a campus classroom, with some of the students in the room and the rest of them at home (which can be tricky; for more on this, see Chapter 7).

Videoconferencing software has a text chat feature, where students can type questions or comments. When you teach synchronously, you should regularly check the chat to see what questions students have posted and answer them as though students asked them in person. This improves the interactivity of the lecture and helps your remote students feel connected to you. If students can ask questions and reply to your questions using their microphones, it's even more engaging, but you'll have to act as a gracious host, making sure students don't talk over each other and that quiet students get a chance to be heard. The authors encourage their students to ask questions and give class contribution credit for asking them.

Webcams showing student and faculty can greatly improve the sense of community in synchronous online sessions. If you can see your students' faces, it'll help you check on how they are doing, just as in the classroom. Students value being able to see their faculty's face, even when you show slides. Students also appreciate being able to see each other, as if they were in an on-campus classroom.

However, some students are uncomfortable showing the insides of their homes or workplaces to their classmates. For example, one of the authors had a student who used to attend his online classes in his car, using a coffee shop's Wi-Fi signal, and didn't want his classmates to know about it—he posted a picture of himself instead. If your students' computers are powerful enough, they can use a virtual background; if they aren't, some students have hung sheets to create a quick background. If this isn't possible, it's still better to include a picture of themselves, rather than just having their name displayed in the picture box.

> Hint: If your students are having problems with their audio or webcam, the chat feature can be used by either faculty or an assistant to help them privately, without disturbing other students.

Teaching an asynchronous class isn't like teaching on campus, because you'll have to have prepared everything beforehand—online web-based lectures, discussion topics, quizzes, and exams—so it can be embedded in the LMS. The good news is that since so much of the work is done up-front, while the course is running you'll have more time to interact with your students.

When it's feasible, we recommend that a web-based lecture contain the most appropriate technology for what's being taught—text, videos, illustrations, animations, interactive multimedia objects, embedded self-assessment questions—and also offer more than one method of instruction.

For example, one of our authors teaches an online course that includes a lot of math problems. There are videos, showing him talking and solving them on a whiteboard, which is best for some students, and they're also displayed in text format, with descriptions of how to solve them. Text is a more flexible format than video, because it allows students to absorb the material at their own pace; it can also be read by **screen readers** for visually impaired students or converted to audio files for students who just want to close their eyes and listen to the lecture (ideally not while driving).

> Hint: We strongly discourage you from embedding a lengthy video of you sitting in your chair talking to the camera. The only thing worse is reading the text from your PowerPoint slides.

3.3 What's a typical week like in an online course?

The basic process of teaching online is similar to teaching on campus. You introduce a topic; teach it in whatever format makes the most sense, all the while asking students questions to see if they understand; summarize it; then assess how well they've learned the material. The difference is how you do this online, with a combination of synchronous and asynchronous methods.

A typical online week begins with an overview of what the students will learn, to establish the scope of the lesson. This can be done with text, but it's easier to inspire your students with a presentation. This can be done either live, synchronously, or asynchronously with a short video.

The advantages of doing the introduction live are that you get a chance to interact with your students, and that it allows them to ask questions. Being in the course live also shows that you're willing to put in the time to meet with students. On the other hand, videos may be used year after year, and they allow you to show students things that may be hard to offer live, such as video of you in a cool location that you couldn't actually be in while teaching. Ideally, you'll have both videos and live introductions, taking advantage of the best of both.

> Hint: You should record your live introductions for students who can't attend.

Most of the rest of the week is spent teaching the content. If you teach your course synchronously, then delivering lectures will be similar to teaching in the classroom. One practical difference is that if you want to hand something out, like a worksheet or a test, or collect papers from students, you have to do it through the LMS.

When a course has asynchronous lectures, these have to be prepared in advance, so successful online faculty spend most of their time in a typical week helping their students by answering questions and leading discussions. Please allow students to ask you questions, as well as have them discuss the material amongst themselves, to address any misconceptions or "holes" in their learning. This can be done in a variety of ways, such as having question-and-answer review sessions or dividing students into small groups to solve a problem, and, if it makes sense, present their answers to the rest of the class. Asynchronous courses have the advantage of letting students reflect more on their answers before answering, and also preventing classroom time from being dominated by a few students.

> Hint: Online faculty need to try a little harder to understand how their students are doing and what they need, because you work with them through computer conferencing software, which is generally more challenging than in person.

While teaching your course, or portions of your course, asynchronously allows many more options to help your students learn, you have to be ready to support students when they use those options. Most asynchronous courses are primarily text, with embedded images, videos, illustrations, interactive objects, self-assessments, and other learning objects. If your students have difficulty learning the material from the asynchronous activities, you should be prepared to provide synchronous activities, such as lectures or Q&A sessions, to help them. One of the ways that faculty can identify areas where their students need synchronous help is by checking the results of the embedded self-assessments while the course is running.

3.4 How many students might I have in an online course?

You might have very different numbers of students in your courses, depending on:

- Program policies, such as course enrollment floors and caps;
- How many students the course is designed to handle; and
- How many faculty and TAs are teaching the course.

The number of students in your course is limited by your institution's and program's policies and the design of the course. You could have a course with only one student, because asynchronous online courses can be designed so that enrollments scale down well. Conversely, you could have a course with tens of thousands of students, if it's designed as a **MOOC**.

> Hint: You'll have plenty of warning if a course is going to be large, because many more things must be done in advance for a course that has thousands of students.

If all you do in your course is lecture at your students, you can have as many students as you want. For example, a speech on TV can have millions of viewers. But, if you want to have any meaningful interaction with your students, you'll be limited in the number of students you can have unless your interactions are automated. For example, in an online course you can include a quiz that provides different feedback, depending on how students answer the questions.

For an interactive course to scale, it's essential that the content be clear and unambiguous, and that the learning activities successfully answer typical students' questions, so you won't have to do it yourself. If there are too many students for you to teach on your own, you'll need help grading the assessments and assignments. Some courses rely on an army of TAs to do grading, and some MOOCs have students grade each other's work. (Caution: Student grading may provide lower-quality feedback.)

Again, some of the help can be automated; for example, automatically graded **multiple-choice** tests are available in all LMSs. If you're teaching an introductory course, many of the answers can be automatically graded, but as you get into higher-level concepts, the students will need your feedback. The more complex ideas get, the more important it is for you to be available to answer questions, guide discussions, and grade submissions.

3.5 How do I make my teaching style clear to students?

Faculty have different ways of interacting with their students and it's important that they signal their preferences, so that their students know what to expect (Cotten & Wilson, 2006). For example, some faculty emphasize synchronous lectures and expect their students to attend, while others don't care if students show up so long as they do good work. If your teaching style emphasizes student participation, this should be reflected in your grading and **rubrics**. (For more on rubrics, see Appendix G.)

If there is a portion of your syllabus which describes you as a faculty member, such as a faculty biography page, you should include information about your teaching style there. You should also make your preferred teaching style clear in your **welcome emails** and introductory lecture.

If your courses have separate pages for faculty bios and contact information, teaching styles can be included there. One of the authors communicates his teaching style in this way:

> I know that some of you may be concerned that this course covers a lot of material. I will conduct Live Classrooms at least twice per week, when you can ask questions, and I will hold one at the beginning of each week, outlining what we will learn and why it's important. I will also go over the assignments with you to make sure that you understand how to approach them and what I expect. When the assignments have been submitted, I will review their solutions in class, using students' submissions (with their permission). While I conduct many live sessions, I don't require that students attend; come when you need to. Because student participation in these sessions helps everyone learn, I may occasionally award a little class participation credit for outstanding questions or discussion.

3.6 How should I dress when teaching online?

One of the common advantages of being faculty is that you have a great deal of freedom about how you dress. Of course, how you dress matters, because it provides your students with social cues that help set the credibility and tone of the course (Dunbar & Segrin, 2012; Roach, 1997). This is true online and in on-campus courses, but online there are fewer social cues, so how you dress when teaching online has more influence than how you dress in the classroom.

Since online education is often perceived as being less formal than on-campus education, if your students need to be reminded to take the course seriously, you may want to dress more formally. Conversely, if students find your course intimidating, it may help them relax if you dress more casually. To maximize credibility with them, dress for the profession you're representing. For example, a banker is more likely to dress in a suit and tie, but a farmer is more credible in a polo or plain t-shirt and jeans (Shoulders & Smith, 2018).

3.7 How can I make my personality come through in online courses?

You may not be aware of it, but you communicate your personality when teaching. This helps your students adjust to your teaching style and expectations. The sooner in the course that the students learn about your expectations, the more it'll help them succeed in your course. In your course introductions, for example, you should be clear about your feelings on things like late submissions and class participation.

The easiest way to share your personality with your students is in synchronous sessions, where they can see, hear, and talk with you. If your teaching style is effervescent, one that encourages conversation and laughter, you'll find this effective in helping your students relax, engage with you and each other, and learn. If your teaching style is more reserved, you may have to make more of a conscious effort to engage with your students.

> Hint: We recommend that everyone use headsets, because this will allow you to talk with your students as you would in the classroom. Without headsets, acoustic noise and feedback may make conversation difficult and unnatural.

Your personality will also come through in your videos; you may even prefer doing them to synchronous performances (a.k.a. lectures). One of the advantages of recorded videos is that you can make them anywhere, so you can take your students on a field trip or show them the view of downtown Boston from your office. If possible, show them things that are related to the subject material that you couldn't show them in a classroom, like a brewery tour for a gastronomy course, or a tour of Boston's Big Dig sites for a megaprojects business course.

References

Cotten, S. R., & Wilson, B. (2006). Student–faculty interactions: Dynamics and determinants. *Higher Education*, *51*, 487–519.

Dennen, V. P. (2005). From message posting to learning dialogues: Factors affecting learner participation in asynchronous discussion. *Distance Education*, *26*(1), 127–148.

Dunbar, N. E., & Segrin, C. (2012). Clothing and teacher credibility: An application of expectancy violations theory. *International Scholarly Research Notices*, *2012*.

Roach, K. D. (1997). Effects of graduate teaching assistant attire on student learning, misbehaviors, and ratings of instruction. *Communication Quarterly, 45*(3), 125–141.

Shoulders, C. W., & Smith, L. (2018). Impact of teacher attire on students' views of teacher credibility, attitude homophily, and background homophily within school-based agricultural education programs. *Journal of Agricultural Education, 59*(2), 275–288.

Chapter 4

Getting more comfortable using online teaching tools

In this chapter we provide more detail about how to use the tools of online teaching, including webcams, microphones, and **videoconferencing** systems.

4.1 How do I set up my workspace for teaching online?

You'll be more successful teaching online if you have appropriate space and equipment, as the physical space that you teach from will affect how your students perceive you. It should be quiet and free from distractions; if you don't have this, a headset can help a lot. Your computer equipment should include at least a device with a good-sized screen, good lighting, and a webcam. Additional equipment, such as a **document camera** and multiple monitors, may be useful in some situations.

During your **synchronous** sessions, your students will probably hear many kinds of background noise from each other; you can minimize this if they wear headsets that have noise-canceling microphones. We don't recommend using a fixed microphone for lecturing, because the volume will vary if you turn your head. A **lavalier microphone** will work in a quiet room. (For more on audio issues, see Appendix H.)

If your computer has USB ports, it'll be easy to connect a webcam or headset. Faculty who do a lot of handwriting or sharing of paper documents may benefit from a document camera. If your computer doesn't have enough USB ports, you can add a powered USB hub. Most faculty who teach online find that a large monitor helps them watch multiple windows without having to change their view. Some faculty have found that two monitors work better.

DOI: 10.4324/9781003161288-4

4.2 How should I set up my camera, lighting, and background?

You need appropriate camera placement, good lighting, and a non-distracting background. The camera should be centered at or slightly above face level. If it's too low, it'll make you look jowly; if it's too high, your students will be staring at the top of your head. Ideally, you should be looking at the camera when you're talking to your students.

We recommend that you use an external webcam, and that you mount it on top of the monitor that you'll be looking at most while you are teaching. If you use a notebook computer, it'll probably have a webcam at the top of the screen, but faculty who use this internal camera may have difficulty keeping it pointed at their face.

> Hint: If you use the camera in a laptop computer or tablet, you can raise the camera by putting books under it.

Your space should have lighting on the front of your face, rather than from above, or your eyes will be in shadow and it won't be flattering. You can arrange good lighting easily using desk lamps; one on either side of your camera will illuminate both sides of your face evenly, without creating nose shadows.

It's best to have the camera and both lamps at the same level as your face, so the light won't make creepy shadows in your eye sockets. The color of the lighting for your face should be warm; lights with a color temperature of 2700°K will work fine. Lights with a bluer ("colder") color will make you look blue and cold—harsh and embalmed.

Students can often be easily distracted, so try to anticipate and avoid problems. For example, try not to have a complicated background, such as busy wallpaper or people working behind you. A plain background—like a blank wall—is better. Some videoconferencing systems let you provide an image to use as a virtual background; this requires a fairly fast computer. If pets or children may interrupt your synchronous sessions, it's a good idea to have someone else watch them, if at all possible.

> Hint: We recommend that you test your camera position, lighting, sound, and background by recording yourself before you teach.

4.3 What technology do I need to learn to teach online successfully?

LMSs create websites, so you should be able to use any device that can render a modern website in your course. You can teach using any sufficiently capable browser, because LMSs are designed to adapt to whatever device you're using. You can even teach using a smartphone (although the small screen makes this slow and awkward, so use them only in emergencies).

> Hint: We recommend that you learn how to tether your computer or tablet to your phone, so you can still teach if your internet goes down or if you don't have internet access when traveling.

The equipment that you need for online teaching depends on what you plan to do in your courses. Table 4.1 summarizes common online activities and the respective tools needed.

Table 4.1 Activities and tools needed for online teaching

Activities	Tools
Using a computer for online access	Computer, internet connection, browser
Videoconferencing with students	Webcam (headset recommended), videoconferencing software
Making slides for online lectures	PowerPoint or similar software
Making videos for demonstrations	Webcam or phone with camera (video editing software recommended)
Showing students what you're drawing, writing, or observing	Document camera, tablet, microscope, or other device for sharing video
Creating and administering online tests	LMS, proctoring software, **lockdown browser**, webcam, proctoring service
Creating online discussions, including blogs, journals, or other forms of discussions	Videoconferencing software (synchronous), LMS, online discussion hosts (**asynchronous**)

So how do you learn to use all that stuff? Most of these skills are transferable from things that you already know. If you already use your LMS to post your syllabus, it's not that much harder to use it to post asynchronous course content. If you use your phone to make videos of your toddler nephew doing the Chicken Dance, you can make videos to demonstrate topics in your courses. You can learn to use these tools by experimenting with them, reading documentation, or watching instructional videos online, but if you get stuck, it's helpful to have someone who can answer your questions. At your institution there are probably colleagues, technical support staff, or

instructional designers to answer questions and demonstrate how to use these tools.

To teach synchronous activities successfully, faculty need to know how to use videoconferencing software, such as Zoom, Teams, or Collaborate. If you don't have enough **network bandwidth** for videoconferencing software, it's possible to teach synchronously using audio and slides. You can teach a purely synchronous course without using an LMS, but you'd be hard-pressed to find a school today that doesn't use one. Students today expect the features provided by an LMS, such as places for faculty to post the syllabus and assignment details, students to submit assignments, and students to communicate easily with each other and faculty.

4.4 What do I need to know to use my learning management system?

When you teach online you mainly use learning management and videoconferencing systems (Reigeluth et al., 2008). Both kinds of systems are fairly easy to use for elementary tasks. If you don't already know how to use your institution's LMS, they probably have tutorial courses for faculty where you can learn the basics. These tutorials will teach you how to:

- sign in;
- navigate within your course;
- communicate with your students;
- insert text and links;
- add images and videos;
- make tests; and
- use the grade book.

To learn more and gain confidence, get a "**sandbox**" copy of a fully developed course, and experiment with it, so you can see how the course was built and how you can change it. LMSs usually have extensive embedded and online documentation, which will help you learn more advanced features. You may also find good video tutorials prepared by the vendors and faculty. If you still have questions, ask people at your institution, such as experienced online faculty, technical support staff, or instructional designers.

> Hint: The best way to find something in the vendor's documentation is to use an external search engine, because it's faster than searching for what you're looking for in the documentation. But you have to learn what things are called by that vendor, because searching on the wrong terms can waste a lot of your time.

Your LMS may not support all the features that your course needs, so you may need to add other software, such as videoconferencing systems, video servers, and student-performance analysis tools. You may be able to link to an external application or website; we use this to provide students access to big-data databases. This has some limitations, such as how to let those sites know who the students are. If external websites offer assessments, such as publishers' assignments, they may require membership to keep track of students' scores, and you may need to pay for access.

For better integration, most LMSs support ways for other software to "plug in" and share data, such as login information and scores. This saves everyone from having to remember usernames and passwords, and the hassle of logging in when going from the LMS to the software (this is called "single sign-on"). Faculty don't normally procure and integrate plug-ins, so you'll need to have the people who administer the LMS do this for you.

4.5 What do I need to know to use my videoconferencing system?

You probably already used videoconferencing systems to communicate with friends, family, and co-workers during the pandemic. Videoconferencing lets you do more things than you can do when teaching in the physical classroom. You'll want to learn to use more advanced features, including:

- recording your sessions;
- using **breakout rooms;**
- giving your students presentation privileges;
- sharing slides, documents, and videos;
- showing your computer screen; and
- muting participants.

Two of the biggest advantages of videoconferencing are that you can record the sessions for your students to review later and that you can create breakout rooms for groups of your students to discuss what they are learning.

You can use breakout rooms in different ways. Think of them as the synchronous equivalent of asynchronous discussion forums. You can create a number of rooms and have all your students go to them to work on a problem or discuss a topic, in smaller groups. If you do this, you should circulate among the rooms to see if the students need guidance.

The other way to use breakout rooms is to create one for a group of students who share a common interest, and run it in parallel with the main session. This can be particularly helpful when students have advanced knowledge of the material, so that the discussions can be at higher levels. This approach has two problems, though: One is that those students are missing part of the main session, and the other problem is that they may need help while you're busy. You can solve these by assigning a TA to work with the students in the breakout room (if you have TAs), and by recording the main session.

The other main advantage of videoconferencing is the ability to record any time you lecture. Whenever you're lecturing using a videoconferencing system, you should record it, so that students who miss the lecture can catch up, and all students will have it available for review. You'll also need to learn how to give your students privileges to share their screens and slides, so they can do presentations. If they use the videoconferencing system for presentations or **study groups**, we recommend that you configure the breakout rooms so that the students can record their own sessions, too. (Be aware that recording student sessions can raise privacy concerns; see Appendix D.)

> Hint: Recording sessions and posting links to them can be complicated, so we recommend that you practice this.

To use videoconferencing well for teaching, you need to learn how to:

- prevent acoustic feedback;
- support students with slow internet (low bandwidth);
- help students get their microphones and cameras working; and
- configure the videoconferencing system.

> Hint: When you're first teaching using videoconferencing systems, we recommend that you invite someone experienced with them to join in and help you and your students get started.

Unless all of your students are using headsets, you'll encounter situations where noise, echoes, or audio feedback make it hard to understand what people are saying. You need to learn how to identify whose connection is causing the feedback and how to mute their microphones. (For more on how to prevent audio problems such as feedback and noise, see Appendix H.)

One of the difficulties of videoconferencing is that video takes a lot of network bandwidth, and some of your students may not have fast enough internet. Videoconferencing systems usually deal with this by slowing the video update rate (a.k.a. "frame rate") for users with slow connections. For example, a student with a slow connection may have their video image turn into occasional updates of still images. In extreme cases, the video may freeze for long periods and look like a lost connection. If your students are videoconferencing veterans, they won't be disturbed by this, but they may still need to be reassured that they'll be able to download the recording of the session.

You'll probably also need to help students with their microphones and webcams when things go wrong. If a student doesn't have a working microphone connection, they can communicate with you using the videoconferencing chat function. The most common cause of microphone or webcam failure is that students haven't selected or enabled them in the videoconferencing system or operating system. You usually can't fix this for them, but you can guide them to fix it. Another common source of these problems is when a student hasn't plugged in their external webcam or headset. Sometimes microphone or speaker problems arise because the volume has been set too low on the headset or operating system.

> Hint: You can learn how to help your students with these problems by experimenting with your own setups, preferably with a second device or a friend to play the role of a student.

Videoconferencing systems have a number of settings that you may need to learn about. You can configure the videoconferencing system so that anyone who knows the URL can log in, and this usually works. Alternatively, if your URL is guessable or has been leaked, you can configure the system so that students need to enter a password; you can also configure the system so that you need to admit each student individually. Other settings can automatically enable students' audio and video when they connect if they're enabled on their computers.

You'll need to assess and balance your security risks and needs. A knitting Zoom group probably doesn't need a password, but a high-school class in a big district probably does.

4.6 Should I use my classroom slides online?

Absolutely! Digital slides remind you of key points you want to make, and they allow you to present material without having to write on a blackboard or whiteboard. Slides are particularly valuable if your presentations include complex diagrams, photos, or graphs. Online whiteboards and other digital drawing tools, such as tablets, may be harder to use than their physical counterparts, so having slides prepared in advance is even more important online than on campus. If faculty make them available, digital slides also help students by removing the burden of writing down their content, allowing students to concentrate more on the lecture, and providing them with a place to make notes of what faculty say.

> Hint: In on-campus courses, some faculty print out slides and hand them out at the beginning of class, so that students can make notes on them during lectures as opposed to trying to copy the slides by hand. If you do this, some students may look ahead in the notes, instead of listening to you. You can reduce this by making slides available further in advance of class and asking questions during the lecture.

If you're teaching synchronously, you can use videoconferencing software with the same slides that you use in the classroom. It's helpful to have a place where all of your slides are posted, so that students know where to find them. If you give slide files logical names that identify the **module** and topic, you can put all of them in one place in the LMS. For example, you could name a slide file "Module 2—The normal distribution."

> Hint: If you teach the same course on-campus and online, it's a good idea to use the same set of slides, to ensure that you cover the same material and keep the courses in sync.

If your course is mainly asynchronous, it's still valuable to have synchronous review sessions where students can ask questions. Review slides are most effective when they summarize the material, instead of merely repeating it. They should only include the major points and most comprehensive diagrams and figures that were used to cover the material during the original lectures.

You can also use your classroom slides as a stepping-stone to developing an asynchronous online course. Figures or other objects in the slides can be included in the lecture in the LMS. Some faculty have had success incorporating their classroom slides in the asynchronous lectures as an introduction to the more detailed text. For example, the original slide could be included as a figure at the top of the web page that has your transcribed text. (For more on creating asynchronous lectures, see Appendix A.)

Faculty have been tempted to record audio over their slides, to save the whole presentation as a narrated lecture. We do not recommend this, because the result is worse than watching a long video. In this format there is no interactivity, and students have to listen to you speak at your usual speed, instead of being able to read at their own speed. A better option would be to record a separate segment for each slide. Even better would be to intersperse **formative evaluations** between the slides, to help students verify that they have learned the material before moving on. This is like asking questions as you lecture! (For more on formative evaluations, see Appendix E.)

Reference

Reigeluth, C. M., Watson, W. R., Watson, S. S. L., Dutta, P., Chen, Z. C., & Powell, N. D. P. (2008). Roles for technology in the information-age paradigm of education: Learning management systems. *Educational Technology, 48*(6), 32–39.

Chapter 5

Designing online courses

This chapter covers the critical planning and course design activities that faculty should complete before they begin building online courses, including making **course maps** and selecting the best **learning activities** and teaching technologies.

5.1 Should I use a publisher's online course, develop my own, or a combination?

Because of the effort required to develop **asynchronous** content, it has become increasingly common for institutions to purchase online courses from publishers or other institutions, sometimes customizing them for their own students.

Courses used to rely on physical textbooks and journal articles, but then the digital revolution began. Publishers originally responded to this sea change by providing supplemental websites for their textbooks, which add animations, sound, video, and **assessments** to the original content. Recently, publishers have shifted to developing online courses designed to be used with their books.

Faculty should consider using these pre-built courses as components or a foundation for their own course **development**, because they reduce development time and effort. Sometimes publishers' tests and other course components can be edited to adapt to your students' needs, but at other times, publishers won't allow this. If a publisher doesn't permit faculty to change its course content, adopting one of its courses is risky, because the content may have errors or other problems that you won't be able to fix.

5.2 How do I get started developing an online course?

Suppose you've been asked to develop an online course. Maybe it's a course that you've already been teaching on campus. Maybe it's a course that you've

DOI: 10.4324/9781003161288-5

been wanting to develop for online. Maybe it's a new course and all you've been given is a simple request, such as "Make an introductory online course on statistics for college freshmen." You may have already chosen a textbook, or not.

If you've already taught this course in person, you've probably already done the following, but if not, you'll need to:

- define the learning objectives and how they'll be measured; and
- decide the order in which you'll teach the topics.

If the course is going to be new to online, you'll have two more things to think about:

- how you're going to teach, asynchronously and **synchronously**; and
- what asynchronous content you're going to build, based on your available time and resources.

When you found out that you'd be developing the course, you probably already started thinking about these things. It's going to be easier to develop if you put your thoughts in a course map, which we'll describe next.

5.3 How do I create a course map?

The ideal way to develop courses is to begin by describing the learning objectives, then determining how you'll measure your students' progress on those objectives, and finally, creating the content that will prepare your students for assessments (Caruana, 2015; Raible et al., 2016).

One of the first things you need to do is to divide your course into **modules** (Woo & Reeves, 2007). The material in each module should be on closely related topics. If you're following a single main textbook, you may wish to align the modules of your course to the textbook chapters, to simplify the course for your students. You may also need to write asynchronous lecture material to supplement the textbook. The course map includes all the information that you would have in lesson plans for on-campus courses, plus descriptions of any asynchronous components that need to be built. Every module of your course should have a **module map**—altogether they make up the course map. The student workload should be about the same for each module. See Table 5.1 for examples of possible content for a module map.

Table 5.1 Possible content of a module map

Component	Description	Hours for students to complete	Example
Module number	Module number	—	1
Module title	Module title	—	The parts of speech
Overview	Provide a general topic and overview of the content	—	In this module we review the essential parts of speech, including nouns, pronouns, adjectives, verbs, adverbs, prepositions, and conjunctions
Course learning objectives	Review your high-level learning objectives for the course (from syllabus). It's okay to repeat them if necessary	—	Students will demonstrate knowledge of English grammar and be able to diagram sentences correctly
Module learning objectives	List specific learning objectives for this week	—	Given an English sentence, students will correctly identify the nouns, pronouns, adjectives, etc.
Prerequisite tasks	Do students need to do anything before beginning this week?	—	Nothing beyond the course prerequisites
Major topic outline	Include the major topics covered this week	—	Nouns, pronouns, adjectives, verbs, adverbs, prepositions, and conjunctions
Required reading	Include book chapters and page numbers, articles, web resources, videos, etc.	1.5	Textbook, Chapter 1; online module 1
Written lectures	Describe what content needs to be written and what learning activities need to be developed	.5	Description and explanation of the parts of speech; exercises in which students label the parts of speech
Media	Describe any videos, multimedia objects, graphics, illustrations, animations, etc. and their functions	.5	Practice for part-of-speech identification: An **interactive object** that presents sentences and asks students to select the part of speech for each word
Individual assignments	Give a brief description of the assignment	.5	Given ten sentences, label all the parts of speech

(continued)

Table 5.1 (Cont.)

Component	Description	Hours for students to complete	Example
Group assignments (if applicable)	Give a brief description of the assignment	.75	Work together to analyze sentences with errors in parts of speech and decide how to fix them
Practice quiz	Include title, number of questions, and format—multiple choice, matching, essay, etc.	.5	A set of questions from which 20 **multiple-choice** questions are presented, in which students identify the parts of speech of words in context. Automatically scored
Quizzes/exams (if applicable)	Include title, number of questions, and format—multiple choice, matching, essay, etc.	.5	A set of questions from which 20 multiple-choice questions are presented, in which students identify the parts of speech of words in context. Automatically graded
Discussion topic or questions	Include whether or not it's a graded discussion	1	How do you use the parts of speech to identify incorrect sentences? (graded) What are the grammar rules for these parts of speech? (graded)
Synchronous session(s)	Introduction: Monday @ 7 PM ET Questions & Answers: Thursday @ 7 PM ET (optional)	2	Introduction to the module Open sessions for student questions
Estimated student module workload		7.75	

> Hint: One reason to include asynchronous components in the map is because developing them can take a long time, and this gives everyone who might be involved in the development advance notice. For example, developing the interactive object in Table 5.1 may require considerable effort.

5.4 How should I order the learning activities?

Different learning activities play different roles in students' learning, so the sequencing of those activities can have a major impact on how well students learn. It is usually best to provide a **study guide** for what students will learn in each module; for example, you may suggest that they read a chapter from the textbook before they study the asynchronous lecture. (For more on study guides, see Chapter 6.)

We recommend that you provide this study guide at the beginning of the module's asynchronous content; you should also encourage students to ask questions about it in the module introduction. Table 5.2 describes our sequence of module learning activities.

Table 5.2 Sequence of module learning activities

#	Learning Activity	Pedagogic Role	Content
1	Study guide	Telling students what's coming so they can plan their studies	Learning activity sequence and due dates
2	Introduction	Inspiring students to study the material and provide context	Asynchronous overview of the main topics in the module, or a synchronous lecture framing the module, where students can ask questions
3	Main content	Teaching the material	Students interact with course material, including media and **formative evaluations**
4	Review session	Reminding students of what they have studied, helping them integrate it, and identifying topics that they need to review	Automatically graded asynchronous review questions with feedback, and/or a synchronous session covering the main topics at review level
5	Discussions	Giving students an opportunity to articulate what they are studying with their classmates	Faculty-created discussion questions, preferably with graded student posts
6	Assignments	Giving students an opportunity to apply what they have learned	Faculty-created solutions, distributed after the due date
7	Quiz	Providing students with an assessment of what they have learned and where they need additional study	A graded, comprehensive test covering the material in the module, preferably with detailed feedback

5.5 How do I want to have discussions in my online course?

The best way to have discussions online depends primarily on your pedagogical goals. Synchronous dialogues are ideal for shorter exchanges, such as answering questions. Asynchronous dialogues are best when students need to research and think for a while before posting, or when you want all students to participate and there isn't enough time to do that synchronously. Common goals and the types of discussion that best support them are summarized in Table 5.3.

Table 5.3 Discussion goals and how to support them

Goal	Type of discussion
Get to know your students	Synchronous or asynchronous sessions
Inspire your students to learn	Synchronous or asynchronous sessions
Let you know immediately if students grasp the material	Synchronous sessions that allow students to ask questions
Help students think in more depth about the subject matter	Asynchronous discussions that give students time to think and research their answers
Make students use vocabulary that they are studying	Synchronous sessions that allow the students to pronounce the words and use them in speech
Collect information from students without requiring that they identify themselves	Asynchronous discussion, with forum options set to allow anonymous posts
Give everyone a chance to participate in a synchronous session	Synchronous sessions
Give everyone a chance to participate in an asynchronous session	Asynchronous discussion, with forum options set to prevent early posters from closing down the sessions by hiding asynchronous posts until everyone has responded, or by having students post and answer each other's questions

> Hint: If students create their own questions, you can keep them on topic by requiring that they cite the relevant areas in the current readings, such as a section in the asynchronous lectures.

5.6 What's a course development plan and how do I create one?

A course development plan is a document that defines the tasks, deliverables, and schedule for building a course. It's essential to tracking development progress and keeping it on schedule. You may be given deadlines by administrators, but you'll most likely need to develop the detailed plan yourself.

The plan should specify dates by which asynchronous lectures and other components must be complete. There may be multiple due dates for one course element, such as when you need to have written a lecture, when the editor or other reviewer needs to finish it, and when an **instructional designer** needs to have it to put it in the course.

One of the main roles of a course development plan is providing a framework to coordinate everyone who's working on the course. The value of a plan and the level of detail that you need increases with the number of people involved and the complexity of the development. Most course development plans are simple documents; a complex plan may be written using a project management tool. Table 5.4 illustrates part of a simple course development plan for a module.

Table 5.4 Part of a simple course development plan

Task	Deliverable(s)	Due date	Responsible person	Recipient
Write module 1 lecture	Word file and any figures	October 20	Faculty	Instructional designer or faculty
Write module 1 introductory video script	Script as document	October 15	Faculty	Videographer
Shoot module 1 introductory video	Raw video footage	October 16	Faculty and videographer	Instructional designer or faculty
Write module 1 quiz	Module 1 quiz implemented in the **LMS**	October 25	Faculty	Instructional designer or faculty
Write module 1 assignment	Assignment and the grading **rubric** as documents	October 26	Faculty	Instructional designer or faculty

To create a course development plan, you'll need the course map, the available resources, and the schedule or due dates. We recommend that you begin your development with a representative module of your course, to understand how long it will take and if there are any difficulties. Your finished course development plan should include all of your modules and all of the course components. For example, your course map may have 14 modules, and each module will have a lecture, a discussion, an assignment, and a quiz.

> Hint: The first module of any course may not be representative of the others, because it has introductory material that the others don't. Therefore, it's usually best to develop a later module first.

We recommend that you develop the modules in order (except for the representative module), for two reasons. First and most importantly, if your course development falls behind schedule and you need to begin teaching your course before it's fully developed, your students can study the completed earlier modules while you finish the later ones. Second, if you have an editor, TA, or someone else to proofread your lectures and other content, they'll also want the material in the order in which it'll be taught.

> Hint: We strongly recommend that you have someone check the material twice, both before it's put in the LMS, and after it's been put in. The first check will catch most errors, when they're easiest to correct, and the second check will catch errors that aren't obvious until the content has been implemented.

You can also use a course development plan to spot schedule risks and keep the development on track. For example, in Table 5.4, if the module 1 lecture isn't delivered to the instructional designer by October 20, this'll delay them from getting their work done.

If (or really, when) there are problems, you should take corrective action, such as delivering part of the lecture synchronously, and try to understand what went wrong to keep the lecture from being done on time. You can also use what you learn in developing the early modules to help you figure this out and plan the others. For example, if it took you five hours to develop the first couple of quizzes, but you had planned for two hours, then you'll have to adjust your plan for the rest of the modules, either allowing more time to build the quizzes or reducing the number of questions in them.

5.7 What's a course template and how will it help me and my students?

A course template is a course skeleton (or "course shell") that contains all of the components that should be in your program's courses. These include the common course navigation, the names and icons of common objects, and common course content such as academic policies and help pages. A course template shouldn't include the content that is unique to each course, such as your lectures, but it should have places to put it.

Templates make courses consistent, which in turn helps students transition between courses (Huun & Hughes, 2014). Once students have learned the components of one course and how to navigate it, they then understand the structure of the others. This reduces the time that they waste learning the organization of each new course, and it cuts down the number of questions they ask.

Templates also speed course development (Newberry & Logofatu, 2008) and make it easier for faculty to develop their own courses. If you put common course components in the course template, you won't have to re-create them each time you build a course. Rather than struggling with the course structure and its technical underpinnings, faculty can concentrate on their content. In some programs, a course template may simply be provided to you to be filled in with your content.

If your program doesn't already have a template, we suggest that one be developed. You can develop a course template by copying a course that has the components and structure you want and then deleting the material that was specific to that course.

5.8 How do I figure out which technologies will best support my learning activities?

Once you have identified the learning activities for your course, you can choose the technologies that you'll use to implement them. For example, if you want your students to discuss a business case in groups, you'll need to choose a technology that supports both discussions and group work. Some learning activities can be supported by multiple technologies. For example, discussions and group work can be done through asynchronous forums or **videoconferencing**.

Some technologies are easy to implement, and some difficult. Often, it's best to start with a technology that is relatively simple and see how well it works, before investing in a more expensive or complex technology. For example, if the learning activity includes a video and you want to test how well your students have learned from it, you can begin by putting a multiple-choice quiz after the video, rather than going to the effort of doing **in-video quizzing**.

Instructional designers are expert in choosing and implementing technologies for learning activities. If you have access to one, we recommend that you consult with them when you have defined your learning activities (for more on working with instructional designers, see Chapter 6).

5.9 How do I decide whether or not to adopt a technology for my course?

You should have a clear reason for adopting a technology or tool (Aldunate & Nussbaum, 2013), besides it being new and promising to "revolutionize" education. You need to know why you want a technology and what you want to accomplish with it. Review your course to identify how you're going to use it and determine where in your course it'll be used.

You may find many reasons for adopting a technology. The most common one is to support a learning activity, such as recording your students speaking Spanish for an assignment. Some technologies, such as videoconferencing, support many learning activities, while others, such as shared whiteboards, have more limited uses. Many technologies, such as discussion boards, interactive formative evaluations, and collaborative tools can improve student **engagement** and learning. Others, such as **lockdown browsers** for proctored final exams, improve **academic integrity** (for more on academic integrity, see Chapter 14).

Sometimes technologies are used in courses to improve students' experience, not specifically to teach something. For example, software that lets faculty attach audio comments to students' papers gives them better feedback and helps them feel more connected.

Tools and technology can improve course navigation, such as having links in test feedback that take students directly to the places in the lectures where that material was covered. Other technologies are designed to help students find things in the course. Some of them would clearly be valuable, but aren't available yet, such as a search engine built into your course that would help students find things in your lectures, video transcripts, discussions, and assignments.

Before adopting a technology, you should ask the following questions:

- Will this technology be around for as long as you want to use it? If the company that provides a technology or service goes out of business or stops selling what you chose, you'll need to find a replacement—will that be possible? What if you can't?
- Who's going to pay for it? Implementing technology in a course may require significant labor. Software licenses may be needed. You'll need to understand the complete costs and who'll pay for them.
- Who's going to support it? Technologies require ongoing technical support. Who'll get the phone call at 2:00 AM when it stops working? If you adopt a technology and no one else wants to use it, you may end up supporting it yourself.

Technology will not make your course better unless you know which ones to use and how they will improve students' learning. You should evaluate the benefits and costs of each technology and decide whether it's worth it. Technology allows us to teach in ways and situations that would otherwise be impossible; we just need to be aware of the costs.

5.10 How can designing for accessibility make my course better?

If you design your course so it's accessible for all users, it will benefit everyone (Oswal & Meloncon, 2014). The most famous example is probably closed-captioning on television programs, which was originally developed for viewers with hearing impairments, but has proven invaluable for watching television across a noisy bar, at home with the sound off to avoid waking sleeping family members, or when it's difficult to understand characters' speech. This approach, treating **accessibility** as something that benefits all users by extending everyone's abilities, is called **universal design**. In distance education, it can not only make your course more accessible to people with disabilities, but also create an environment that can be used to the greatest extent by the most people, regardless of their abilities (National Disability Authority Centre for Excellence in Universal Design, n.d.).

For example, if a website only differentiates items by color, these objects may be indistinguishable to people with color blindness. You can address this by distinguishing items in multiple ways, such as labels, positioning, variations in typeface, or patterns and backgrounds. This will not only help people with color blindness, but also be understandable if printed on a black-and-white printer.

Try to build course elements so that they have many uses (Wynants & Dennis, 2018). If your course presents material as text, students will have more ways of studying the material than they would have with just video or audio. Text and video transcripts should be in a form that can be read online, printed, saved as a file, or read aloud by the user's computer. Students can read the transcript rather than watch the video, have their computer read the text file to them, or listen to the transcript while exercising, walking, or driving. Ideally, videos should include closed captions as well as transcripts that can be searched, downloaded, and read aloud.

When building pages in the LMS, you should:

- Make page titles using the title text area instead of just making the text large and bold, because the LMS will add header HTML tags that **screen readers** use.

- Ensure that colors and their saturation have high contrast against their backgrounds, so that they print clearly and can be easily read by people with color blindness.
- Offer alternative ways of presenting the material. If you have video, include a transcript, closed captioning, and descriptive text. If you're adding an image to a course in the LMS, fill in the **alt attribute** description field that's provided, so students using screen readers will know what the image is.

You don't need to implement all universal design principles at once to make your course more accessible. You can add universal design features when it's convenient. For example, if you're making your own videos, you can attach the script that you used as a transcript when you add the video to your course. If you don't know how to add closed captions, they can be added later by someone else.

References

Aldunate, R., & Nussbaum, M. (2013). Teacher adoption of technology. *Computers in Human Behavior, 29*, 519–524.

Caruana, V. (2015). How a course map puts you on track for better learning outcomes. *Faculty Focus* Retrieved 18 January, 2021, from www.facultyfocus.com/articles/course-design-ideas/how-a-course-map-puts-you-on-track-for-better-learning-outcomes/.

Huun, K., & Hughes, L. (2014). Autonomy among thieves: Template course design for student and faculty success. *Journal of Educators Online, 11*(2), 1–30.

National Disability Authority Centre for Excellence in Universal Design (n.d.). *What is Universal Design.* Retrieved November 1, 2019, from www.universaldesign.ie/What-is-Universal-Design/.

Newberry, B., & Logofatu, C. (2008). An online degree program course template development process. *MERLOT Journal of Online Learning and Teaching, 4*(4), 583–595.

Oswal, S. K., & Meloncon, L. (2014). Paying attention to accessibility when designing online courses in technical and professional communication. *Journal of Business and Technical Communication, 28*(3), 271–300.

Raible, J., Bennett, L., & Bastedo, K. (2016). Writing measurable learning objectives to aid successful online course development. *International Journal for the Scholarship of Technology Enhanced Learning, 1*(1), 112–122.

Woo, Y., & Reeves, T. C. (2007). Meaningful interaction in web-based learning: A social constructivist interpretation. *Internet and Higher Education, 10*, 15–25.

Wynants, S., & Dennis, J. (2018). Professional development in an online context: Opportunities and challenges from the voices of college faculty. *Journal of Educators Online, 15*(1), 1–13.

Chapter 6

Developing asynchronous elements of online courses

We cover the creation of **asynchronous** online lectures in Appendix A; in this chapter we answer questions about how to develop the other asynchronous elements of online courses. We address **study guides**, videos, collaboration tools, and working with **instructional designers**.

6.1 What's a study guide and how do I create one?

A study guide is a table listing the things that students need to do, and when they're due. They differ from typical syllabi schedules because they are organized by **modules** or weeks to provide a checklist of things due during that period. Study guides list due dates and times for assignments, discussions, **assessments**, and **synchronous** sessions. Guides may also recommend that students do things in a certain order, such as read a textbook chapter before that module's asynchronous lecture.

It's helpful for students to have study guides in both the syllabus and the modules. We list study guides for all the modules together in the syllabus, so that students can easily get an overview of the entire course on one web page. Each module also displays its study guide, typically at the beginning, to show students what they need to do soon. Table 6.1 shows a typical module study guide.

You can maintain syllabus and module versions of your study guide as separate documents, but we don't recommend this, because it increases your work and introduces the possibility of inconsistencies.

The authors use a few lines of JavaScript in the **LMS** to automatically link the study guide that is displayed in a module to the original in the syllabus. Then, when a course runs again, only the syllabus study guide needs to be changed to update the ones in the modules. This saves time and prevents mistakes every time we update courses, so ask your institution's technical people about the best way to do this with your LMS. We use this to update hundreds of courses a semester, but it's still worthwhile for just a few.

DOI: 10.4324/9781003161288-6

Table 6.1 A typical module study guide

Module 5: The Larger Social Level
Tuesday, August 3–Monday, August 9

Required Reading/ Viewing Discussions	• *Principles of Psychology*, Chapters 10 and 11 • Module 5 online content Module 5 discussions • Initial posts due Wednesday, August 4, 9:00 AM ET • Two peer replies due Sunday, August 8, 9:00 AM ET • Summaries posted by the week's student group leaders due Monday, August 9, 9:00 AM ET
Assignments	Research paper outline due Thursday, August 5, 9:00 AM ET
Live Classrooms	Saturday, August 7, 7:30–9:00 PM ET
Activity	Module 5 review-and-reflect essay due Monday, August 9, 11:59 PM ET

6.2 Why should I make videos for my course?

Good videos can add energy to your course, but bad ones can put your students to sleep. Nobody wants to watch videos of people sitting and talking for hours. The last thing you should do is record yourself talking for two hours, throw it into the LMS, and call it an online lecture.

How do you decide when or if you need a video? Videos should be used when they are the best way to present the material:

- demonstrating physical skills, such as knitting or surgical techniques;
- taking students to places where they couldn't go, such as a tour of the space station;
- showing students what they can't see by normal-time observation, such as time-lapse videos of flowers opening, or a building being constructed; or
- showing faculty working through a problem solution so students can see how the steps are done, such as simplifying an equation.

Unless the video is the centerpiece of the asynchronous lecture, start with text, and then ask yourself which parts would benefit your students most by being shown as video. The best approach is to present critical content in multiple formats, such as both text and video.

Your students will be more involved if you prime them to watch the videos by setting their expectations of what they'll learn. Videos should be as short as possible and focused on only one topic, so that students can review them when studying without having to wade through irrelevant material (Lagerstrom, Johanes, & Ponsukcharoen, 2015). If a video needs to include multiple topics, it can be broken into shorter videos or segmented into chapters with a table of contents. For example, if it's a video of someone being interviewed, each chapter can be of them answering a different question. If possible, you should also include transcripts of videos, so students can read along and search, and for **accessibility** reasons.

Measure how useful your videos are by using the facilities in your LMS and video server to see if your students watch the videos, if they finish them (and if they don't, see how far they get), and if they watch them more than once. You can also learn if your students find your videos engaging—or how they could be improved—by asking about them in surveys or **student evaluations**.

> Hint: We examined our video server logs over a period of several years, and found that students simply stop watching most videos after about six minutes—or even less, if the material is repetitive.

6.3 How do I make videos for my course?

How you make videos depends primarily on the available resources. At one extreme are faculty who may only have a cell phone or notebook computer with basic video editing software, and at the other are faculty who have access to a studio with videographers and video editors. No matter how your videos are made, there are a number of things that you need to do:

- plan what you're going to say and write it down to remind yourself—a.k.a. use a script;
- keep your videos short—less than ten minutes—and on one topic;
- use good microphones and a quiet room so students can understand what you're saying;
- use lighting that helps you look good;
- edit your video to eliminate dead time and errors; and
- make captions and/or transcripts.

If you have access to a studio with videographers, make sure that you send them your script at least a day before the recording session, so that they can load it into the teleprompter (if they have one). Your script can be written out word-by-word, or, if you're comfortable speaking in front of a camera, it can be just a series of bullet points.

> Hint: If you make a mistake reading your script, stop, take a breath, and start again from the beginning of the paragraph or bullet point. Video editing can cut out the mistake and no one will know.

Watching a video is a lot slower than reading; you can't skim a video like text. Consequently, you should design your videos so that they are short and make good use of your students' time.

Add closed captions and transcripts to your videos, both because they support students with disabilities, and because they let all students skim and search the text of the video. Closed captions and transcripts also help students understand faculty with wicked Boston accents.

There are several ways to create captions and transcripts:

- upload the raw videos to a transcription service;
- have them transcribed automatically by software and then clean them up; and
- type them yourself or pay a student worker to type them.

Video content can be made more interesting—and you can avoid student fatigue—by changing how it's presented. You can do this by moving the camera angle, finding new filming locations, or inserting other clips. This technique is used a lot in television news. For example, when a person at the scene of a newsworthy event is being interviewed, they don't just show the person talking; they intersperse those shots with video of the scene.

You can also make your videos more captivating by asking your students questions. The simplest way to do this is to ask questions in the video and pause while they think of their answer. You can also do **in-video quizzing**, where the video stops, a question is presented, and students select an answer. If they answer correctly, the video continues; otherwise, the video goes back to where the topic was covered. If you don't want to do in-video quizzing, you can break your video into a series of shorter videos and embed them in the LMS, with **formative evaluation** questions in between. (Geri et al., 2017).

When you've got the raw footage, you (or the videographer) should edit your videos to cut mistakes and dead time. Video editing software is readily available for download; you may already have some on your computer. Editing your videos gives you a second chance to eliminate unimportant material that wastes your students' time.

6.4 Should I use augmented reality and virtual reality when teaching online?

Augmented reality (AR) and **virtual reality** (VR) are technologies that provide the user with visual and other information that enhances or replaces what they may normally see, hear, or feel. AR superimposes computer-generated imagery and sounds over the natural imagery and sounds around the user. VR uses computer technology to replace natural imagery, sounds, and even touch, so that people have the illusion that they're someplace else.

AR and VR both require technology that senses where you are and where you're looking. Fortunately, many smartphones have this technology, so they may be all that students need for basic AR and VR. This is what enabled the Pokémon Go AR game to become popular in 2016.

AR's most useful when teaching skills that involve a student exploring their environment, with the support of overlying imagery and narration. For example, in a consumer education course, students could point their smartphones at products in stores, scanning UPC barcodes, and the AR system could tell them about the environmental sustainability of each product, and the carbon footprint of the company overall.

In a math course, AR has helped students visualize abstract concepts, improving math learning and satisfaction (Chen, 2019). AR allows "trigger images" to display illustrations, video clips, or hints as extra sources of information. Or, imagine that you're teaching a chemistry class, where you need to cover the shape of a molecule. AR can display a 3D rendering of the molecule in the students' hands and give them the illusion of grasping and rotating it as they learn its structure.

There are several challenges and concerns with adopting AR:

- Effort is needed to create digital objects, but that's getting easier as the software matures.
- It can be difficult to cue the digital presentation trigger image to where the student is, and where they point their device. For example, if you're creating an AR session for an art class, you could make the trigger image a certain painting, that when scanned with the device reveals more information about the artist. This is easier to do with two-dimensional objects, like a painting, than three-dimensional objects, such a statue that you can walk around. You can put the trigger image that activates the AR on a webpage in your LMS.
- Real imagery may be transmitted to the servers of the organization that provides the technology, which raises privacy concerns (Pesce, 2020). You can minimize these risks by having the AR be in a public space, like a park.

Faculty need to balance these challenges and security concerns against the advantages of including such technologies in their courses.

VR has traditionally been used when teaching skills that involve simulating a realistic environment surrounding a student physically doing something, such as flight simulation, physical therapy, or performing a medical procedure. VR can also take students on tours of places that they couldn't realistically visit, such as the inside of a beating heart, where the students have the illusion of walking through it as though it were a series of rooms, pausing to examine structures they're interested in. In this, VR allows students to interact with things more deeply than if they were watching a video, which can increase **engagement** and learning (Dede, 2009).

An emerging use for VR is to represent complex things as simple objects, so that students can concentrate on how they interact, just as people often find it easier to solve a text-based logic puzzle if they make a sketch of the relative position of objects and their attributes before they focus on the relationships between the objects ("The person with the red hat arrived before George, who did not have the yellow coat"). For example, a game was developed to teach object-oriented programming, in which text details of functions are hidden, but the connections and flow of data between functions can be modeled (Kao et al., 2020).

There are significant challenges when using VR in teaching. One is the sheer effort needed to create digital environments for VR; publishers and other companies are beginning to provide virtual environments and technologies, so that's getting easier. Another is the cost of VR headsets, since VR usually requires that users wear a headset to create the illusion of three-dimensional vision. These headsets currently cost about as much as an inexpensive smartphone, though the cost is coming down. A final, perhaps most concerning issue is cybersickness, motion sickness brought on by virtual environments or simulators, in which some users experience nausea and dizziness. While cybersickness has been an issue since the dawn of VR, it is expected to become even more prevalent with the recent proliferation of VR headsets (Yildirim, 2020).

> Hint: Consider encouraging your institution's library to have headsets that students can check out like books.

6.5 How can I use collaboration tools to improve communication?

One of your responsibilities as faculty is to facilitate communication and learning, and the right tools can make that easier. Collaborative tools help you integrate group work and problem-solving into your courses. Because they record who has contributed to group projects—and what—they help address the age-old problem of grading each student fairly. The common types of collaboration tools and how they improve communication are listed in Table 6.2.

Table 6.2 Common type of collaboration tools and how they improve communication

Type of tool	How it improves communication
Communication tools, such as Slack, help students keep in touch with their classmates and work groups.	Your students can use these to share documents and coordinate activities within groups.
Project- and task-management tools, such as Asana and Trello, allow students to organize group activities.	Your students can use these to assign and track tasks to ensure that nothing falls between the cracks and that projects are done on time.
Collaborative authoring tools, such as Google Docs, allow students to create and edit documents together. These include **wikis**, shared word processing, and checklists.	Your students can use these to create joint project reports. This'll allow them to see each other's contributions and comments, saving many email and file exchanges.
Source control systems, such as GitHub, support distributed software development.	Your students can use these to develop software cooperatively, with version control.

> Hint: Some of the functionality of these tools can be implemented in LMSs, but their versions tend to be relatively weak. If you need more capable tools, choose them carefully, because you don't want to have to switch tools in the middle of a course.

6.6 How can I develop my online course to include student projects and presentations?

There are many kinds of student projects, and many ways of doing them online. When developing a course that has projects, you need to decide:

- How many projects will there be?
- Are these individual or group projects?
- Will there be presentations and, if so, how will they be implemented?
- How will projects and presentations be graded?

You may decide that your course would be best with two projects, one due before the midterm and one due at the end of the term. In this case, your students probably won't get too far behind schedule, so reminders from you should be enough to keep them on track. If your course has only one, large term project, your students may get behind and not be able to catch up, so we recommend milestone deliverables to motivate students and help them stay on schedule.

> Hint: You could assign equal weight to the report and presentation, or you may want to adjust the proportions of weights for different projects. For example, a project that develops an advanced animation would naturally weight the presentation more than a highly theoretical project.

You'll then need to do the following things to prepare your course for student projects and presentations:

- write a document that defines the term project or projects;
- write the project-grading rubric;
- create milestones for deliverables and provide assignment drop boxes;
- create a video that teaches students how to do presentations;
- create a **videoconferencing** practice room; and
- create enough presentation rooms to allow for concurrent presentations.

Before your students present, we recommend that you provide a videoconference **virtual room** where they can practice. This will allow them to learn how the videoconferencing system works, how to record their sessions, and how their presentations will appear to their audience.

If you have many students in your course, term-project presentations may take a lot of time. You can manage this by limiting the maximum length of the presentation, and by scheduling presentation sessions that extend beyond the ordinary class time. TAs may need to attend and grade the presentations. (For more on working with and ensuring fair grading with TAs, see Chapter 9.) The presentations should be recorded, and your TAs should tell you if you need to review any of the recordings.

If students are divided into groups, you should consider asking that group members attend their classmates' presentations. You can encourage this by giving a little course credit for good contributions to the discussion.

Academic integrity can be an issue in presentations, so if your students know that you'll be attending their presentations and asking questions, this will discourage them from having other people do their projects for them. You should record their presentations in case you need them as evidence, and run their submissions through an **originality checker**. (For more on academic integrity, see Chapter 14.)

6.7 How can I develop an online course in a hurry? Can't I just record my regular lecture?

The main challenge of developing any online course in a hurry is developing its asynchronous content. (For more on creating asynchronous lectures, see Appendix A.) You can speed the **development** by building only the essential asynchronous content and/or by having other faculty or publishers provide it. Most of the work in developing an asynchronous course is creating the written lectures, so if you need to do it fast, plan to teach most of the material synchronously and to focus your resources on the parts that need to be asynchronous: tests, assignments, and discussions.

Here are two techniques that you can use to speed the development of the first draft of your asynchronous lectures. One is to pretend that you're lecturing in the classroom and make a transcript using videoconferencing or other software; edit it, and then enhance it with slides from your presentation. This won't be just a narrated PowerPoint, but annotated text, which lets you insert formative evaluation questions to make the experience more valuable for your students. This will help meet diverse student learning needs. (For more on accommodating student differences, see Chapter 12; for more on formative evaluations, see Appendix E.)

> Hint: Automatic transcription will introduce errors, so you should always proofread and correct it.

If you have both the faculty resources and the **course map**, the other technique is to have different faculty develop different modules of an asynchronous course. If several faculty are writing different modules, they each need to be able to see what the others are writing, so the terminology and style are consistent. This also helps faculty make sure that each module prepares students well for later modules, covers all necessary topics, and avoids repetition.

> Hint: If several faculty are writing a course, you should plan to review what is written to make sure that it all fits together. Be sure to allow time for this.

6.8 How can instructional designers and other staff help me?

Faculty decide what to teach, and skilled staff can help them develop materials to teach it well online. Most faculty don't have much experience creating online courses, or other work that requires a lot of technical help, so working with instructional designers, videographers, animators, and editors may be new to you. If you have access to any of these staff, consider yourself fortunate, because they'll make your life easier and your course better:

- Instructional designers will suggest ways in which your teaching concepts can be improved and implemented.
- Videographers will help you make high-quality videos for your course; they may edit your videos or even record you in a studio.
- Animators will help translate your napkin sketches into fancy graphics.
- Editors will help ensure that the way you say things is consistent, and may even help you say what you mean.

Different programs provide different levels of support for faculty:

- In programs with a great deal of faculty support, the faculty write the content and instructional designers and other staff implement it.
- In programs with less support, the faculty create everything except videos and advanced **learning objects**, which may be created by specialists.
- In programs with minimal support, faculty do everything by themselves, though instructional designers may provide technical support.

6.9 How can I work most effectively with instructional designers?

To work most effectively with an instructional designer, you need to understand that they have ways of thinking about courses that are different than most faculty, and that their ways of thinking are helpful in producing a good online course. Fundamentally, designers have studied the practice of designing courses that help students learn; most faculty have not studied this material, but they need it to develop effective online courses. Try not to be defensive when an instructional designer suggests potential changes to your courses, and try to understand how those changes may help your students. Academic freedom applies more to *what* we teach rather than *how* we teach it; designers can't help us in what we teach, but they should be experts in how we can best teach it online.

How you work most effectively with your instructional designer depends on their role, or roles in your program and on your recognition of how they can help you. Different programs use designers in surprisingly different ways. In some, designers play a relatively minimal role, serving mainly as training and technical support in helping faculty implement their own courses.

In other programs, designers are far more involved, working closely with faculty early in course development, helping them design the course elements, and helping them choose the best methods for attaining their learning objectives. In such programs, designers implement what faculty write and integrate learning objects created by others, and they may also coordinate the other staff, such as editors, videographers, illustrators, and animators, throughout the entire course development project.

"Implementing a course" includes uploading files to the LMS, creating links, building tests, setting grade-book calculations, and building multimedia objects. Faculty often think of courses as no more than the text files they create. Instructional designers think of online courses as websites, with pages, navigation bars, and other website components, such as videos and animations. They also may improve the uniformity of the design of courses across a program; it helps students learn when course navigation and the location of elements are consistent across courses.

Different programs have different processes for developing, implementing, and reviewing courses; you should know the preferred process for your program and support it. Be aware that you should plan to complete your writing early enough to allow time for reviews and changes. Faculty reviews are best performed before the content is put in the course, because it's easier to make changes. You should also have at least one review after your content is implemented, to catch bugs in layout and function.

References

Chen, Y.-c. (2019). Effect of mobile augmented reality on learning performance, motivation, and math anxiety in a math course. *Journal of Educational Computing Research, 57*(7), 1695–1722.

Dede, C. (2009). Immersive interfaces for engagement and learning. *Science, 323*(5910), 66–69.

Geri, N., Winer, A., & Zaks, B. (2017). Challenging the six-minute myth of online video lectures: Can interactivity expand the attention span of learners. *Online Journal of Applied Knowledge Management, 5*(1), 101–111.

Kao, D., Mousas, C., Magana, A. J., Harrell, D. F., Ratan, R., Melcer, E. F. et al. (2020). *Hack.VR: A Programming Game in Virtual Reality*. https://arxiv.org/pdf/2007.04495.

Lagerstrom, L., Johanes, P., & Ponsukcharoen, U. (2015). *The myth of the six-minute rule: Student engagement with online videos*. Proceedings from 2015 ASEE Annual Conference & Exposition.

Pesce, M. (2020). Augmented Reality and the Surveillance Society. *IEEE Spectrum* Retrieved December 19, 2020, from https://spectrum.ieee.org/computing/hardware/augmented-reality-and-the-surveillance-society.

Yildirim, C. (2020). Don't make me sick: Investigating the incidence of cybersickness in commercial virtual reality headsets. *Virtual Reality, 24*(2), 231–239.

Chapter 7

Developing and teaching blended courses

This chapter describes the issues involved with teaching **blended** courses, in which students attend some sessions on campus and others online. It describes how blended courses are different from purely on-campus or online courses, and how blended courses can be a stepping-stone in developing purely online courses.

7.1 What's a blended course?

In a blended (or **hybrid**) course much or all of the material is available online, and there are also meetings on campus (Welker & Berardino, 2005). Blended courses typically have less on-campus meeting time than traditional on-campus courses; consequently, you should do what you easily can online and save the precious on-campus time for activities where it's most beneficial. Table 7.1 lists common blended formats.

Strictly speaking, on-campus teaching only allows faculty interaction during class time and office hours. Now that most faculty are reachable via email, on-campus courses have taken on an aspect of online courses, in that students can interact **asynchronously** with their faculty at any time.

It's easier if you can start by teaching blended courses before you teach fully online, because the on-campus portions of the course will be familiar. You'll get to know your students in the on-campus sessions, and you'll be able to give them quizzes and exams during those sessions, so you won't need to worry about the **academic integrity** challenges of purely online courses. (For more on academic integrity, see Chapter 14.) Because you'll be meeting with your students face to face, you'll be able to identify students who are anxious, and be able to help them; you can do this online, but it's more difficult. (For more on working with students who may need extra help, see Chapter 11.) The online portion of a blended course brings with it all of the advantages of online, including allowing students to study from

DOI: 10.4324/9781003161288-7

Table 7.1 Common blended formats

Blended format	Classroom attendance	Website content
Some required on-campus sessions	Students are required to attend on-campus classes on certain days, typically for **assessments**, group **learning activities**, demonstrations, labs, and presentations	Most of the course material is online
Flipped classroom	All students are required to study online before coming to on-campus class	Most of the course material is online
Telepresence	All courses are taught on campus; students are expected to attend either in person or online	Varies
À la carte	Students can attend any number of on-campus classes, or none	All the course material is online

anywhere at any time. Blended courses are the best of both worlds for faculty with classroom experience who are new to online.

Some subjects, such as chemistry, lend themselves naturally to a blended format, where the theory is covered online, and the labs are done in the classroom. Blended formats can be designed so that fewer students may be in a classroom at the same time; this can be helpful if there's a shortage of classroom space, or to allow social distancing.

Blended formats also work well when students or faculty can't make it to the classroom. If most or all of the content is online, and there is an opportunity to meet on campus, the courses can be much more robust than courses taught purely on-campus or online. For example, if a course cannot be held in a classroom because of bad weather or a pandemic, you can hold the classes online. If students don't understand something online, like the proper angle to hold a calligraphy pen, it can help to work with them in person.

Blended courses can help you improve asynchronous online material. When teaching a blended course, you may wish to present new or particularly difficult material both asynchronously online and **synchronously** on campus, because then your students can ask questions and provide immediate feedback, and you can go back and improve the asynchronous lectures. (For more on creating asynchronous lectures, see Appendix A.)

7.2 How do I use my online course materials in a "flipped" course?

A flipped course is a type of blended course, in which the students study the material online and then come to a physical classroom to discuss the material.

It is called "flipped" because in a traditional lecture class the students learn the material in the classroom and then practice it in homework assignments. Flipping works well because it makes the best use of technology to prime students and the best use of classroom time, when students engage with each other and their faculty on what they have studied (Roehl et al., 2013). Labs may also be done in the on-campus parts of a flipped course.

> Hint: Traditional teaching contains elements that are like flipped classes without technology. You can revert to this if you don't have online asynchronous content, by having students read textbooks or papers and discuss them in class.

If you already have an asynchronous online course, you can use those materials as the online portion of your flipped course. (For more on creating asynchronous lectures, see Appendix A.) There are a couple things you may need to do to prepare your course for flipping:

- Add readiness assessments to help both students and you understand whether they have completed their online study assignments and are ready for the classroom.
- Modify quizzes and tests so that they fit in the classroom format; for example, a three-hour final exam may need to be broken into three one-hour exam segments.

In flipped courses, faculty usually take advantage of having their students in the classroom for tests and occasionally for assignments, which can address the problem of assuring academic integrity and proctoring. (For more on academic integrity, see Chapter 14.) If you build your tests in the **LMS**, you can take advantage of features like question randomization and automatic grading; this can reduce your grading effort. (For more on automatic grading, see Appendix E.)

7.3 What's different about teaching a blended course?

If you're teaching a blended course, you need to prepare for both on-campus and online activities (McCown, 2010). This involves deciding which activities and materials work best in the classroom and which online. A well-designed blended course can take advantage of the best characteristics of both modes of teaching.

> Hint: Every time you create a slide for your on-campus course you can also use it for your online course materials. Slides will be more effective for online students if you include what you would say in the classroom.

Even though you're in the classroom with your students, they'll also expect you to be with them for the online portions of the course. You should monitor your in-course messages, email, texts, etc., and respond promptly, or carefully manage your students' expectations about how often you'll be online and how quickly they can expect a response. Ideally, when you teach a blended course, you should go into the online portion of the course every day, because online and blended students usually expect faculty to check in at least once per day, and often every morning and evening (Hailey Jr. et al., 2001; Zhang et al., 2016).

One of the differences between online and blended teaching is that you need to design blended courses to fit into existing course and on-campus schedules, which are less flexible than online. For example, our authors usually ask their online students when they would like to have synchronous sessions, and they conduct them when the most students can come; this is not possible on campus, because classrooms must be scheduled, and meeting times published, long in advance. If some of the material has to be taught on campus, you may need to change the sequence of the **modules** to make your course fit around the existing class schedule.

If you're just starting out and don't have access to online proctoring, you may want to conduct some of the assessments on campus. For example, you may have your students take quizzes online but have them take their exams on campus under your watchful eye.

7.4 How much effort does it take to prepare and teach a blended course?

How much effort it will take you to prepare and teach a blended course depends on how much of the course will be taught online, whether the online parts will be taught synchronously or asynchronously, and whether or not you'll need to develop the asynchronous content (Gedik et al., 2013).

If the online portions of the course are taught synchronously, the preparation is the same as if you were teaching on campus. Online synchronous teaching itself will be similar to teaching on campus, except that it will be done through **videoconferencing**.

If the online portions are taught asynchronously, the amount of effort it will take to develop that material will vary. Developing asynchronous content can require considerable effort, and you may need to acquire additional skills, such as how to use the editing tools in the LMS. (For more on developing asynchronous online content, see Chapter 6.) If you need to develop a lot of the asynchronous content, the preparation workload will be significantly greater the first time the course runs, but you should do it before the term starts, and then you can use it again and again.

If good asynchronous content for an online course has already been developed, then you can prepare it for a blended course with little effort, although you'll need to ensure that it fits with your classroom schedule. (For more on creating asynchronous lectures, see Appendix A.) If your blended course has regular on-campus meetings, such as once a week, then little rearrangement of the material may be necessary. If your blended course has few on-campus meetings, then you may need to rearrange the schedule of the online materials so that key on-campus activities, such as exams and labs, fall on the right days.

It's much easier to adapt the content of an existing online course for a blended format than it is to develop that content. It will take less effort to teach a blended course that is based on a fully developed asynchronous online course because the asynchronous content will help students learn the material, so you won't have to answer as many questions and help as many struggling students. A prerequisite review module in your asynchronous content will also help. (For more on creating a prerequisite review **Module 0**, see Appendix B.) If the assessments have been designed to be automatically graded, this will further reduce your workload while the course runs.

7.5 How do I transition my on-campus course to blended?

The easiest way to transition an on-campus course to blended is to teach the synchronous online portions of your course just as you would in the classroom, using videoconferencing (Singleton, 2012). One of the big advantages of starting with synchronous content is that you can gradually replace it with asynchronous material. This will give you a place to insert images, animation, and **interactive objects** as you gradually learn where they are needed and how to build them.

You should start by building online components that have a high return on your time investment and that are easily implemented asynchronously, such as assignments, assessments, and discussions. Once they're in the course, this will save you time when you teach the course in the future. (For more on creating asynchronous lectures, see Appendix A.)

We recommend converting your on-campus course material to asynchronous online material in the following order. Start with items that you probably already have for your on-campus course and which are easy to put in the LMS. These first items are low effort with a high return:

- assignments,
- quizzes, and
- discussions.

The next items require high effort and provide high return:

- written lectures and
- **formative evaluations** and review questions.

Finally, there are items that take relatively low effort, and the return depends on how important they are for your course:

- student presentations and
- tests and final exam

Table 7.2 provides more specific guidance on how to convert common types of on-campus learning activities to a blended course.

Table 7.2 On-campus learning activities and how to adapt them for a blended course

On-campus learning activities	How to adapt them for a blended course
due date reminders	Post in the online syllabus; when students are on campus, remind them what's coming.
introduction to a topic or module	Video your on-campus introduction to topics, to insert in your course for later iterations. Be sure to allow synchronous time for your students to ask questions.
lecture about the course content	Reinforce asynchronous lectures with on-campus interactions. Start by delivering synchronous online lectures, which you record to make transcripts to build asynchronous lectures. Improve these by embedding images from your slides, videos, and other **learning objects** as you build or acquire them.
demonstration	Record and present demonstrations online, unless it's important for your students to experience a sense like smell or taste that can't be conveyed through video.

Developing and teaching blended courses 67

Table 7.2 (Cont.)

On-campus learning activities	How to adapt them for a blended course
case studies	Decide whether they'll be provided in the LMS or if students need to buy them, like books. Be aware that case studies may have specific licensing issues.
debate	Decide whether debates will be held online or on-campus, synchronously or asynchronously. For asynchronous debate, have your students upload time-limited videos or word-count-limited text. For synchronous debates online, with large classes and TAs, create a videoconferencing **breakout room** for each TA, to allow more than one debate at a time.
discussion	Reinforce asynchronous online discussions with synchronous on-campus discussions.
guest lectures	Invite guest lecturers to the online portions of your course, so they'll not have to come to campus.
in-class labs	Do labs online when feasible. Chemistry and other labs that require special apparatus and materials may need to be on campus.
students asking questions during a lecture	Give your students options. Asynchronously, they can ask questions through email and discussion forums; synchronously, they can ask questions in videoconferencing, either verbally or through text chat. Students can signal that they have a question by using the **"raise your hand" function**.
problem-solving/ brainstorming	Asynchronously, use discussion forums. Synchronously, use videoconferencing. If the course is too large to have good videoconferencing discussions, conduct multiple sessions with different students or divide students into groups with TAs, using breakout rooms.
projects	Provide ways for groups to communicate and work together online: asynchronously with discussion boards and collaboration tools, and synchronously, with videoconferencing rooms.
review sessions	Reinforce asynchronous review online with synchronous review, either online or on campus. Ideally, use automatically graded self-assessments with feedback for asynchronous review. If you can't, provide review questions and their solutions asynchronously.
roleplay, seminars, question sessions	Use videoconferencing, and record for grading and review.
field work, site visits	Field work is the same in a blended course as it is on-campus. Site visits to local sites are also the same. Show sites that students can't easily travel to using video recordings or live videoconferencing.

(continued)

Table 7.2 (Cont.)

On-campus learning activities	How to adapt them for a blended course
student presentations with student and faculty questions	Conduct student presentations synchronously and ask students questions to help ensure academic integrity. In larger classes, have students present to subgroups, rather than the whole class.
take-home quizzes/ assignments	Post, collect, and return asynchronous assignments online. Allow time to answer questions about the assignments and their solutions both online and on campus.

7.6 How do I use a blended course to develop a fully online course?

A blended course gives you an excellent place to start from when developing a fully online course. A number of the course elements should already be in the LMS, and you already know what you'll want to say in the asynchronous lectures.

To bring a blended course fully online, you'll need to do a number of things:

- Ensure that you have a capable videoconferencing system, since you'll rely on it for synchronous communication.
- Decide what you're going to do in synchronous online sessions, and how often you'll have them.
- Adapt all of the on-campus learning activities to online.
- Convert the synchronous lectures in your blended course to asynchronous.
- Update your syllabus to reflect the new online components and due dates.
- If TAs are used, they should be introduced to your students in the syllabus.
- Include pages for technical support, online policies and procedures, and links to your institution's or program's general online orientation.
- Arrange for the proctoring of exams, and possibly other assessments.

7.7 How do I teach with some of my students on-campus and some online?

Teaching on campus when some students are present and some are remote requires that you divide your attention between these two groups. This takes some practice, but technology can make it easier and more effective.

The most basic technology setup for this situation is when faculty use the camera, microphone, and speaker built into a laptop. This works well when the on-campus students can sit around the laptop to see what's going on, hear, and be heard. If you have too many students in your classroom to fit around your laptop, then you should add external speakers, an external camera, and a microphone. Your remote students will also be able to hear and see better if you use external devices. If you use a large monitor or screen on campus, your students can see remote students who use webcams.

The most challenging aspect of dividing your attention is knowing when your remote students have a question or need your attention. They can ask questions using audio or text, and you should let them know how they can best get your attention or ask to speak. If you use the "raise hand" feature of videoconferencing systems, you should ask your classroom students to help let you know if a remote student raises their hand. This also helps encourage communications between on-campus and online students.

You may need to help some remote students become and stay engaged (Venton & Pompano, 2021). If remote students use webcams, and you show their video feeds in the classroom, then all students will feel more connected. In small courses, you can improve the **engagement** of remote students by having them introduce themselves at the beginning of the first class. If they aren't participating as much as you'd like, try giving them priority in responding to your questions and even directing questions to them. Of course, all students will be more involved if faculty ask lots of questions and encourage them to respond.

> Hint: Some faculty keep track of how many times they call on each student. This can also be used to tally how many times they call on remote and on-campus students, to ensure that they call on all students equally.

7.8 How do I encourage communications between on-campus and online students?

Here are three techniques for encouraging communications between on-campus and online students:

- Make it easy for them to talk in the classroom by arranging for good audio and video.
- Have online activities for everyone.
- Have them work together in teams or groups.

Classroom and remote students can speak with each other if those who are remote have their microphones enabled and they can be heard clearly by everyone in the classroom. This works best if your remote students use headsets. In addition, you need to have enough microphone coverage in the classroom so that the remote students can hear what is being said. (For more on audio, see Appendix H.) On-campus and remote students can see each other if the remote students use webcams and you have a webcam in the classroom that shows the students.

> Hint: If you have two devices, such as a laptop and your phone, one can be pointed at you and the other can show your on-campus students.

A well-developed course includes asynchronous and synchronous activities that enable dialogue between on-campus and online students. With asynchronous activities, such as discussion, students don't even know who's remote and who's based on-campus. You can also enhance the communication between both kinds of students by conducting synchronous online sessions where you ask lots of questions and encourage dialogue. The best kinds of discussions are those where students do most of the talking. (For more on synchronous sessions and asynchronous discussions, see Appendices C and D.)

You can also encourage communication between remote and on-campus students by forming teams or groups that include members from both groups. If some in the group meet in person, and others want to meet online, it's easy to bring a laptop to a physical meeting to include the remote students. They can also form teams that only meet online.

References

Gedik, N., Kiraz, E., & Ozden, M.Y. (2013). Design of a blended learning environment: Considerations and implementation issues. *Australasian Journal of Educational Technology, 29*(1), 1–19.

Hailey Jr., D. E., Grant-Davie, K., & Hult, C. A. (2001). Online education horror stories worthy of Halloween: A short list of problems and solutions in online instruction. *Computers and Composition, 18*(4), 387–397.

McCown, L. J. (2010). Blended courses: The best of online and traditional formats. *American Society for Clinical Laboratory Science, 23*(4), 205–211.

Roehl, A., Reddy, S. L., & Shannon, G. J. (2013). The flipped classroom: An opportunity to engage millennial students through active learning strategies. *Journal of Family & Consumer Sciences, 105*(2), 44–49.

Singleton, D. M. (2012). *The transition from traditional to blended on-campus learning experience*. [Unpublished doctoral dissertation]. Nova Southeastern University.

Venton, B. J., & Pompano, R. R. (2021). Strategies for enhancing remote student engagement through active learning. *Analytical and Bioanalytical Chemistry, 413*, 1507–1512.

Welker, J., & Berardino, L. (2005). Blended learning: Understanding the middle ground between traditional classroom and fully online instruction. *Journal of Educational Technology Systems, 34*(1), 33–55.

Zhang, C.-W., Hurst, B., & McLean, A. (2016). How fast is fast enough? Education students' perceptions of email response time in online courses. *Journal of Educational Technology Development and Exchange (JETDE), 9*(1), 1–11.

Chapter 8

Teaching online courses

In this chapter we describe what you need to do when your online course is running.

8.1 How long should my synchronous lectures be?

One of the differences between **synchronous** teaching in the classroom and online is that maintaining attention online is harder (Beard & Harper, 2002); failing to recognize this generally leads to frustration. In the classroom, students can do lots of things to help them deal with fatigue. For example, they can make eye contact with their classmates, look around the room, or concentrate on different aspects of what the faculty are doing. Students get tired faster in synchronous online sessions, so you should conduct shorter and more frequent sessions.

In addition, the attention span of students generally increases as they mature (Richardson, 1994). Undergraduates may only be able to learn effectively from lectures for about 40 minutes. Graduate students can usually maintain their attention for about an hour. Most faculty who teach longer on-campus classes learn to have breaks about once an hour; your online students need the same, only more frequently. If you need to conduct a synchronous session longer than about an hour, we recommend that you have periodic breaks.

The breaks needn't be time when you're away from the session; your students just need a change to refresh their attention. For example, you can tell your students that you're going to have a break where they can step away from their computers or talk with their classmates, or you can stay to answer questions. (Recommendations for the lengths of different kinds of synchronous activities are in Appendix C.)

DOI: 10.4324/9781003161288-8

> Hint: Any unexpected change will help your students maintain their attention. Changing a slide won't do it, but something as simple as taking your jacket off or telling a relevant story will.

8.2 How do I schedule synchronous lectures for my online course?

Sometimes the times of the synchronous lectures are published with the course sections so that students can make sure that they'll be available. In other cases, it works better to leave the scheduling decisions about synchronous lectures until the faculty can determine when students are able to attend. This can be done before the course opens, or in large courses, by using polling tools such as Doodle. After the course opens, you can use polls built into the **LMS** to have students select a day and time that works best for them.

If your course is small enough, you can combine the polling with an **asynchronous** discussion about when synchronous sessions should be held. This ensures that everyone has an opportunity to voice their preferences.

Often no single time can be found that all students can attend. We have found that two sessions per week will accommodate most students. This approach can also help students who need to attend both sessions to learn the material well. In large courses, having multiple synchronous lectures covering the same material reduces the number of students in the sessions, so that they can participate better in the dialogues. If none of these strategies work, students who can't attend a synchronous session can watch a recording.

8.3 How many hours will I need to spend on synchronous instruction each week?

The number of hours you spend each week interacting synchronously with your students depends on the subject matter, how well your students are doing, how well the asynchronous content of the course has been developed, and where you are in the course.

You'll need to spend more time with your students in courses where interacting with their faculty is essential, such as those at the master's or PhD level; in these you may need to spend several hours per week. If your asynchronous content is well developed with **formative evaluations** that answer students' questions, you may need to spend only two or three hours per week. (For more on formative evaluations, see Appendix E.)

> Hint: You should plan on conducting at least one hour of synchronous teaching per week, plus one or two office-hour sessions that last as long as your students need to get their questions answered.

You can help students who are struggling by conducting additional synchronous sessions where they can ask questions. (For more on helping struggling students, see Chapter 11.) You'll need to budget more time for this in newer courses; in fully developed ones, your students should be able to answer almost all of their questions from asynchronous lectures, formative evaluations, feedback in review questions, and feedback in **assessments**.

Students' need for synchronous communication with their faculty is highest early in the course and near the end. Early in the course, the students are working to understand what the course covers, as well as faculty expectations and teaching style. Near the end of the course, students will be wrapping up their assignments, submitting any late work, and preparing for the final exam. If your course has term-project presentations, your students will also be doing these in the last week or two of the course.

> Hint: Consider conducting synchronous review sessions before the final exam, in which you cover the highlights of the course and welcome questions.

8.4 How and when do I do discussions online?

Discussions are an important part of learning for most students, and they should be incorporated at appropriate points within the course **modules**. Online discussions can be synchronous or asynchronous. Synchronous discussions are similar to those in the classroom; the difference is that online synchronous discussions are conducted with **videoconferencing** systems. (For more on how to conduct synchronous sessions, see Appendix C.) Your online course should have discussions associated with each learning objective, as one of the **learning activities**.

When you're developing your course, the best approach is to include asynchronous discussion questions in each module and also to conduct synchronous question-and-answer sessions (Vonderwell et al., 2007). We recommend that you conduct a synchronous discussion session for each lecture or module, where students ask questions, and everyone participates. This helps you build relationships with your students and allows you to answer questions for everyone at once, rather than separately.

Asynchronous discussions are the most common type of interaction in online courses, and they have no counterpart in on-campus classrooms. They allow more students to participate, even simultaneously (Comer & Lenaghan, 2013). Asynchronous discussions are usually implemented using LMS discussion tools, but social media can also be used (for more on using social media, see Appendix D). Discussions are similar to comments that you see on websites; there are lead posts created by faculty, and then students comment on them and on each other's posts.

Discussions can be most useful to students at different stages in their study of a given topic. Some students like to read the discussion questions before they study the lecture material, to learn what they need to be able to discuss and the questions they'll need to answer. Other students prefer to study the material first, and then turn to the discussions, to articulate what they have studied and to identify areas where they need to learn more.

Asynchronous discussions usually begin with questions posed by faculty. The best questions are derived from learning objectives, and encourage students to explore topics more deeply. They should be open-ended, so that many students have an opportunity to respond to the same questions. For example, a history professor could ask, "Given what we've studied in the 19th century, do you think nationalism has been a force for good or evil? Discuss, please." We recommend that you have more than one question on each topic and allow students to respond to any of them. Then your questions are less likely to be exhausted by early responders and there are still opportunities for later responders. (For more on asynchronous discussions, see Appendix D.)

You may be accustomed to giving some grade credit for contributions to on-campus discussions, and you can do the same for both asynchronous and synchronous discussions. You'll need to create a discussion grading **rubric**, so that your students will know what's expected of them (Hew et al., 2010). (For more on rubrics for grading discussions, see Appendix G.)

> Hint: We recommend that you consider a rubric which awards credit to students for posts based on how much they contribute to their classmates' learning.

8.5 When should faculty participate in online discussions?

Your primary role in online discussions is to post seed questions and guide student learning. When a discussion forum has many pedagogically useful posts, and it stays on topic, you may not need to participate, but you'll need to monitor discussion forums to be sure that they're staying productive. If you provide multiple discussion questions that cover the learning objectives, more students can participate. Some students may be reluctant to post, so you may need to encourage them.

The primary reasons that you need to post are if a discussion:

- strays away from the learning objectives;
- has offensive or otherwise inappropriate posts;
- dies down before important topics have been covered;
- is stagnating and you think that it's time to change the topic;
- is missing responses that you expect;
- contains incorrect information that other students don't correct; or
- topic hasn't been summarized well by students.

(For more on both synchronous sessions and asynchronous discussions, see Appendixes C and D.)

8.6 How do I perform assignment reviews and solution walkthroughs?

In disciplines with a heavy emphasis on problem-solving, faculty may choose to go over assignment requirements in a synchronous session, and solicit questions to make sure that students understand what's expected and how to approach the problem. You should do assignment reviews when you think that students may have difficulty approaching a complex assignment. You can discuss the assignment rubrics in this session. (For more on rubrics, see Appendix G.) In many courses the assignments may be well tested, and the students well enough prepared, that this is not necessary.

In an assignment-solution walkthrough, a student presents their solution to the class in a synchronous session. Solution walkthroughs are most helpful for advanced assignments that have multiple or complex solutions. The assignments should be graded, so that the students can see the faculty feedback. Faculty should usually choose which students' assignments are presented, based on their pedagogic value. When feasible, faculty should choose diverse solutions that illustrate both the range of possible answers and pedagogically useful errors. If your students are having difficulty adjusting to your grading standards, it can also be helpful to choose outstanding solutions, to show what's expected.

Assignments in online courses must be unambiguous and detailed; students must know exactly what's expected of them. On-campus students can ask questions in class and faculty can answer them just once; online students will send you many emails seeking clarification. Inevitably some students will have questions, which you should address in a synchronous review.

8.7 How do I make assignments more interactive for online students?

Sometimes assignment interactivity helps students learn skills that they can't learn on their own. Assignments can be interactive if the student interacts with other students, a computer system, or both. For example, a group problem-solving assignment can work well when teaching students how to address complex problems, because the group interactions will help them understand that there are different ways to think about problems and their solutions. As students work together to solve a problem, they'll learn from each other as well as the assignment itself.

> Hint: A course can be made more enticing to some students by making some assignments more like games. **Gamification** can draw unmotivated students into a course, but it doesn't necessarily improve interactivity.

Group work is most effective when the problem-solving requires nuanced reasoning and there are complex or multiple solutions. Group problem-solving can be asynchronous or synchronous, though synchronous sessions foster more spontaneous, engaging dialogue. We suggest that you provide rubrics so that students know what you value and how you'll grade; rubrics should address both students who don't participate enough and those who dominate. (For more on rubrics, see Appendix G.)

Some courses lend themselves to team projects, which can be intensely interactive. Team term-length projects can have larger scope than students can undertake by themselves, so they can be used to give students experience solving problems of the scale and complexity that they may encounter in future jobs. Large team projects should be divided into tasks that can be performed by individual students, and those tasks should have well-defined, gradable deliverables. There should be synchronous team meetings at least once per week, with faculty in attendance, and the meetings should usually be recorded, so that students can review them and faculty can use them for grading.

> Hint: Faculty may sometimes intervene in a team project to enhance learning, such as reassigning students to different tasks or changing the project requirements.

One highly interactive synchronous activity is roleplay. For example, in a clinical psychology course, a candidate therapist works with classmates who play the roles of clients, and the faculty provide guidance and feedback. Every student takes their turn acting as the therapist. This kind of highly interactive activity provides students with direct experience in what they'll be doing in their practice. Roleplaying activities may be applicable any time students are learning how to interact with other people.

An assignment can also require students to work with **interactive objects** in the course. For example, suppose that an assignment in a finance course asks students to spend pretend money on five Dow 30 stocks of their choice. Later, the financial simulation tells the students how they and their classmates did. Sophisticated objects can be more interactive, asking questions about the students' stock choices, such as how a company's debt burden is likely to affect its short- or long-term stock valuation. Developing pedagogically useful interactive objects for assignments may require that faculty anticipate and create responses for common student actions, which in turn requires an investment of faculty and developer time. The effort is justified if many students will be working on an assignment.

Some of the most powerful types of interactive objects are those that provide a realistic simulation of a system that the students need to understand, or the interaction of multiple systems. For example, medical students learning how to help diabetics control their blood sugar levels can be helped a great deal by a simulation where students control patients' medication, when their blood sugar is measured, and what they eat. Physicians can gain the skills they need through experience interacting with the simulation, without any risk to actual patients or having to wait in real time to see what happens (Beck, 2019). Similarly, a flight simulator is very helpful in aerodynamics courses, enabling students to experience phenomena such as stalls and spins safely.

In some courses, assignments can be designed that require students to interact with people in their community or things in their environment. For example, students in a social work course may be asked to interview homeless people to identify ways that they can be helped. Sometimes interaction may involve observations, such as when ecology students take water samples from a local pond and analyze them. This can particularly enrich online courses, because students in a single course can collect data from different geographies and cultures.

8.8 How do I know if my online course content is interactive and engaging?

For your students to learn, they need to be intellectually engaged with what you're teaching (Chen et al., 2008). A good way to engage them is by creating courses that are highly interactive, so your students become active learners. There are a variety of techniques for assessing whether your course content is interactive and engaging.

If possible, ask experienced online faculty or **instructional designers** to review the interactivity of the course when you're planning and developing it. During the **development** process, you can make sure that interactive components are on every page.

Once it's running, you can give your students surveys or mid-semester reviews to ask if they found the course engaging. For example, you can ask them, "Did the group problem-solving sessions help you understand the material better? Would you like to do more of them? How can we make them better?" If you want your students to think about the questions and respond at length, it's best to collect this data asynchronously. If you want more of your students to respond and engage in a discussion, you should collect this information in synchronous sessions.

> Hint: Asking students to complete lengthy surveys takes time away from their studies, so don't ask them to spend much time on them; it should be obvious why you're asking. When feasible, have just one survey in a course and make it short enough so they can respond to it in less than 15 minutes. Make the response to your surveys optional, so only students who feel strongly about the questions will respond to them.

You can also learn from **student evaluations**, which are often administered at the end of courses. These are typically designed to cover all courses, so you can compare them. However, there may not be specific questions about **engagement**, so you may need to infer it. Evaluations also won't include questions that are specific to your course. For example, your course may have a new **learning object** and you want to know if your students found it engaging. You can gather this from an in-course survey, but you may not get it from student evaluations. Most evaluations do include space for text responses that may provide insight into how engaging students found the course, and ways to improve it.

It's fairly easy to see whether your synchronous sessions are interactive and engaging: Record your synchronous sessions and measure the interactivity. How many times do you ask your students questions? How many times do your students ask questions? How much time do they talk as opposed to you? (Hillman, 1999)

Studies have shown that faculty consistently underestimate the amount of time that they spend talking and overestimate the levels of discussion in their courses (Alvermann et al., 1990; Conner & Chalmers-Neubauer, 1989). If you find that you're spending more than a few minutes at a time talking at your students rather than the students doing most of the talking, then your lectures are not as interactive as you can make them.

The most interactive synchronous sessions are driven by student questions and comments. You can tell how engaged your students are by the frequency and relevance of their questions and comments. If your students always come to your sessions eager to participate, then you know they're engaged. If they don't want your synchronous sessions to end, and ask you to continue, you know that they're engaged, or you're having a very good dream. (For more on how to conduct synchronous sessions, see Appendix C.)

> Hint: Some faculty try to force their students to come to their synchronous sessions by assigning course credit for attendance. We don't recommend this, because attendance is not a measure of learning. If you find that your students aren't coming, we recommend that you make your synchronous sessions worth their while, so they will.

Synchronous sessions can also help you learn how engaging your asynchronous content is. If your students complain that the asynchronous material is dry or dull, then you know that it needs work. This sort of communication is easier in the more casual environment of a synchronous session.

You can also check the LMS's student activity reports to see how much time they spend studying asynchronous material online and where they spend it in the course. For example, if you have formative evaluations that tell you how many times students try them, you can see if students are skipping some questions. (For more on formative evaluations, see Appendix E.) If students aren't answering particular questions, you should try to make them more useful and interesting.

8.9 How do I fix non-technical problems in my online course?

First, you need to determine if the problem in your course is of a technical nature, or due to content that doesn't meet your students' needs. You or instructional designers can easily correct many of the minor technical problems in your course, such as broken or misdirected links. (For more on diagnosing and fixing technical problems, see Appendix I).

Most non-technical problems in courses can be corrected by changing, updating, or adding new content. Common examples include:

- editing the text in a lecture so students can understand it better;
- updating a quiz question that students found unclear;
- updating an assignment to make it clearer;
- adding a discussion forum in an area of current interest;
- adding a formative evaluation in a portion of your lecture where students are having trouble, so they can test their knowledge;
- adding a video illustrating how to do something; or
- adding or updating feedback to quiz questions.

The best time to fix problems in your course is before it's open to students. They prefer to feel that courses are stable, and not changing randomly while they're taking them. There are exceptions, such as when you add material about a current event or emerging technology, or respond to student requests; these changes help students feel that you're responsive to their needs.

You can change content that the students can't see yet at any time, including while the course is running. For example, if you're teaching Module 2, and there's something you want to change in the Module 4 quiz, which isn't open yet, you can do so without students knowing.

> Hint: Changing assessments while a course is running can be problematic, because students will be concerned that others will be graded based on different versions of problems. Most LMSs won't let you modify a test once a student has taken it.

If you're changing content that students may have already seen, such as the written lectures for the next module, you should let them know what you've changed and why. For example, if you've added a new section on an emerging topic, you should let them know so that students who've already studied the lecture can go back and read that new topic. If you're in a situation where new content needs to be added and you don't have the time to write asynchronous content, we suggest that you cover it in a synchronous session, which you record, and then use the transcript to build asynchronous content when you're able. (For more on creating asynchronous lectures, see Appendix A.)

8.10 How much should I communicate with my students when I'm teaching online?

When course development is rushed or done poorly, subject material can leave students with many questions, so they may need to interact with faculty frequently. By contrast, in a well-developed course, with strong asynchronous content and opportunities for students to interact with their faculty in scheduled synchronous sessions, relatively little unscheduled interaction may be necessary.

We recommend that you have an introductory synchronous session at the beginning of each module, to frame the material for the week and to reinforce a personal connection with your students. These sessions needn't be lengthy; a ten-minute introduction may be more than enough. It's also important to have a review and question-answering session near the end of the module. If there are few questions during your question-and-answer sessions, and your students are understanding the material, these sessions can also be short.

> Hint: You should tell your students that you are recording the question-and-answer sessions for them to review. These recordings can also help you when the time comes to update the course, to remind you what course material needs to be improved.

One of the advantages of online education is that students can have access to their faculty many times during the week, and not just in class. You should ask your students to email you using only the internal email in the LMS, and use your regular email only as a backup. This keeps your students' email from being buried under the usual avalanche of regular email.

Internal email is also archived with the course, as a permanent record. You should check it at least once per day, because students may have urgent, private communications, such as that they are ill. It's also important to set students' expectations about how frequently you'll respond to email. For example, if you're planning to check your LMS email in the morning and evening, you should let your students know that in the syllabus.

> Hint: In general, texting between faculty and students is not recommended, because there's no audit trail and the texts don't get archived with the course.

8.11 How do I manage online "office hours"?

Online office hours differ from on-campus, because many students can be in a videoconferencing system at once; there's no office door to close, and no row of chairs in the hallway where they can wait.

We recommend that you schedule office hours in your online courses at least once per week and publish those times in the course calendar. Office hours should be conducted using videoconferencing tools when possible, and you should use a webcam to build rapport with your students.

> Hint: If your videoconferencing or internet connection fails, you can still meet your students for office hours by using a phone conference call.

When students are in many time zones, try to schedule office hours that are convenient for everyone. For example, many of our selfless faculty schedule office hours at 10 AM ET and 7 PM ET on Saturdays, so that everyone is awake for at least one of the sessions. These regularly scheduled, published office hours are best conducted as question-and-answer sessions, where students ask questions and you and other students discuss and answer them.

Online office hours are easier to attend than on-campus, and students can work on other things while they listen. Consequently, you're more likely to have many students show up at the same time. When this occurs, try to see if many of them have the same issues or questions, which you can address at the same time.

Our faculty usually conduct office hours where everyone is invited, and they record the sessions so that those who can't come can view the recording. If students have issues that need individual attention, you should arrange to meet with them in private sessions. For example, if a student is stuck on an assignment, they can share their partial solution with you in a synchronous session. Private office hours between you and one student should not be recorded, because you may be discussing how they are doing in the course and what they can do to succeed.

In office hours, the students control the agenda by the questions they ask; in a lecture, faculty control the agenda. Online, office-hour sessions can turn into supervised discussions, when a student asks a great question and everyone has something to contribute. If some students monopolize the session, preventing others from participating, you may need to manage who you call on with questions.

8.12 How should I provide feedback to my online students?

How you provide feedback to online students depends on the situation and the information that you need to convey, and that will affect how much of your and your students' time it takes. Prompt feedback speeds learning and improves student satisfaction (Carless et al., 2011).

If the feedback requires extensive back-and-forth dialogue so that you can both explain what you mean, then a synchronous session will be more efficient than email. If a student doesn't understand your initial asynchronous feedback, such as your comments in a graded assignment, then it's helpful to ask them to join you in a synchronous session via videoconferencing or phone. Table 8.1 summarizes common situations and faculty responses.

Communication with students that requires a legal record is best done by email, using the email function in your LMS; the transmission is guaranteed and the message will be archived. One example is when you must confront a student for plagiarism. Another example is when you need to warn a student that they are not doing well in the course or that some of their behavior is unacceptable. Asynchronous communication gives students more time to think about your questions and formulate their response. If you need to tell someone something that may be upsetting, it's a good idea to send the message asynchronously, to give them time to cool off and write a reasoned response.

Many kinds of feedback to individual students are more effective synchronously, because they give you and the student an opportunity to discuss whatever you're talking about efficiently. Talking also conveys feelings and strengthens relationships in ways that asynchronous communications don't. If you want to help a student who struggled with an assignment, you may invite them into a private videoconference where you share and discuss their submission. If you want to learn how your students are doing, you talk with them, listen, and work from there.

Table 8.1 Common situations and faculty responses

Situation	Your response
A student asks an easily answered question in email or chat	Reply to the student's email or chat
A distressed student asks for help	Invite the student into a phone call or private videoconference session
A student asks a question that requires a complex reply	By email or synchronously, depending on the nature of your reply
A student asks a question that is likely to require a lot of back-and-forth communication	By synchronous communication so that you can both figure out what the other means
A student is suspected of plagiarism	By email, so you have a record of your communication
A student posts something inappropriate	A discussion post, carefully correcting the student
A student is unable to understand the grading of an assignment	Your rubric should explain the grading. If the student still has questions, review them in a synchronous session. In some disciplines, you may also conduct assignment-solution workshops, so your students will understand how to solve the problems.
A student complains that their score on an assignment is too low	Share anonymized exemplary assignments

8.13 What should be the tone of my email with my students?

Your email should always be polite and professional, no matter what you're responding to, or how you feel. Imagine that your email is evidence in a court of law. It should be clear, unambiguous, as short as feasible, and well organized. When writing to a student, you should try to begin in an affirming way, although this has limits. For example, "I am confident that you can write a fine term paper on your own, but I have evidence that some of the paper you submitted was not your own writing."

Consciously think about your tone when emailing students. Imagine that you're in your student's shoes; read your email, and consider how it would affect you. Always keep this in mind before you click "Send." Recipients of email often interpret it as more negative or neutral than intended (Byron, 2008), so it's usually a good idea to festoon the email with more friendly indicators than adults would generally use in personal correspondence. (One of the authors prefaces email with a casual "Hi [Whoever]," and uses exclamation points to convey enthusiasm. The exclamation points are discomfiting, but effective.)

If it's obvious that one of you isn't understanding the other, don't be afraid to use a private videoconference or phone call to improve the communications (Hailey Jr. et al., 2001).

> Hint: Writing is a great way to express your feelings, but it's better to do this in a word processor rather than your email program, to avoid accidently sending a rant.

8.14 What are the benefits of communicating with online students before and after courses run?

The primary reasons to communicate with your online students before their course opens are to help them prepare for it and to begin establishing your relationship with them. It's more difficult to establish and sustain a sense of connection with students online, so starting early gives you more time to get to know each other, and shows that you're taking the initiative to reach out to them.

> Hint: This is a good approach for traditional, on-campus courses as well.

A good practice is to email your students several weeks before the course launches; this will give them an opportunity to make sure that they have the correct textbook and to begin studying. If your course has prerequisites, you should make this clear in the emails and let your students know that they should reach out to you if they haven't met them.

We recommend that you email your students at least three weeks before the course launches, and every week thereafter, until launch (you should also resend the emails to students who registered late). These emails should include a welcome to the course, the syllabus, prerequisite requirements, faculty contact information, and guidance on how to prepare for it. You should also make a particular effort to encourage students who feel unprepared to contact you. As the launch date approaches, students may want more specific information to help them prepare, such as an extract of the first module and the early assignments.

> Hint: If your course has a lot of reading, your students will appreciate receiving the syllabus in advance so they can get a head start on it.

Once the course has ended, reaching out to your students after the grades are in gives you a chance to show that you care about their academic and professional success. You can do this using email. We recommend the following content:

- thank them for taking your course;
- ask them to stay in touch with you and each other; and
- wish them the best in their professional and personal lives.

8.15 What are some of the practical advantages for faculty of teaching online?

On a more personal level, teaching online has many advantages for faculty, including the ability to teach from anywhere (Li & Irby, 2008). As long as you have internet access, you can travel when you're teaching a course, rather than being forced to stay close to campus. Even when you're staying home, it's easier to fit appointments into your calendar, because online activities can be rescheduled more easily than in-person ones—they're not affected by traffic or weather conditions, and there's no need to worry about running all over campus for back-to-back appointments. There are also significant financial and health advantages to teaching synchronously from home and further advantages to teaching asynchronously.

At home it may be easier to concentrate, because there are fewer work-related interruptions. In addition, when you work from home it's easier to take advantage of small chunks of time to do your work or interact more frequently with your students, and you can more easily accommodate late-night and early-morning student interactions. You can also interleave work with household chores or spending time with your family.

You may also be able to save money by teaching from home. You'll have no commuting or parking costs, and you won't need to spend time commuting and hunting for a parking place. This is especially important for adjunct faculty who have to travel to multiple institutions, or full-time faculty who teach at multiple locations. You can also save money by eating at home and making your own coffee. During the pandemic, many people realized that they only needed an appropriate "Zoom shirt" for meetings and could save on office clothing. If you have young children, you may be able to keep an eye on them while performing asynchronous tasks, such as grading, saving on the cost of childcare; however, you may want a separate space where you won't be interrupted during synchronous sessions.

There are also some less obvious health advantages of teaching online. During the pandemic, many teachers have observed that they didn't get colds or flu because they weren't spending time near contagious students, faculty, or staff. This is particularly important for people who are at high risk from infections. Another health advantage is that if you're mildly ill, you can teach from home and don't need to go to campus where you may infect other people; you'll also be able to care for yourself better at home.

Finally, if you're working from home you can rest when you need to. Teaching online gives you more flexibility to schedule the length of your synchronous sessions, which can have health benefits in addition to being easier for many students. If a three-hour lecture is too tiring for you or your students, you may be able to offer it as three one-hour sessions without having to worry about finding an available classroom.

8.16 What are some of the practical challenges for faculty who teach online?

The first challenge of teaching online is learning how to do it (Palloff & Pratt, 2011). Our faculty who have learned to teach online love it and so do their students. Perhaps the biggest challenge in teaching online is how much of the work needs to be done in advance. If you're the type who likes to have everything ready to go at the beginning of the term this is fine, but if you like to take a more freewheeling approach, you may have trouble.

Another challenge of teaching online is the effort required to develop asynchronous content. There are usually somewhere between 25,000 and 50,000 words of asynchronous lecture material in our typical graduate-level courses, to give a sense of the effort required. Students will expect the written lectures to be of textbook quality, so you should write carefully and have someone review your work.

You'll also need to create tests and assignments that will work online. If you've taught the same class on campus, you should be able to reuse or adapt the assignments and tests; they'll just need to be implemented in the LMS, so your students can do them online. This is straightforward, but can be time-consuming, even when you've learned how to use your LMS. (For what you need to learn about your LMS, see Chapter 4.)

On a more personal level, if you work from home, you won't have many of the resources that you would have when working on campus. You may have slower internet at home and may have to share your **network bandwidth** and other resources with family members. When things go wrong, you won't have in-person technical support. You'll need to set up a quiet place with good lighting to teach your synchronous sessions (a "**Zoom room**"), and you won't have access to many school amenities such as gyms, coffee shops, and health clinics.

There is also the lack of spontaneous social interaction. This has many ramifications, including increased difficulty establishing relationships with your colleagues, students, and staff. You'll miss out on gossip, meetings with food, and birthday parties with cake.

8.17 Will teaching online advance my career as faculty?

It depends. If you're at a school that values teaching, developing your online teaching skills will help you become more valuable, be in greater demand, and have more job security (Green, Alejandro, & Brown, 2009). When faculty learn to teach online, they hone their course development skills, such as the best way to organize courses, how to create good discussion questions, how to write good lectures, and how to create automatically graded tests with question randomization. Online faculty also learn to think about how they teach and interact with their students. All of these skills can also be used when you teach on campus, making you a more effective and versatile teacher.

One of the advantages of being a skilled online faculty is that there are more opportunities to teach online than on campus, because many online programs are growing rapidly. Unfortunately, many on-campus programs are struggling to maintain enrollments, and some have even been forced to lay off faculty. Because you can teach from anywhere, you can accept teaching positions far away from home without having to relocate. When you teach online it's easier for you to work at more than one institution or part-time while you're working another job; this can facilitate your transition to full-time teaching.

References

Alvermann, D. E., O'Brien, D. G., & Dillon, D. R. (1990). What teachers do when they say they're having discussions of content area reading assignments: A qualitative analysis. *Reading Research Quarterly, 25*(4), 296–322.

Beard, L. A., & Harper, C. (2002). Student perceptions of online versus on campus instruction. *Education, 122*(4), 658–663.

Beck, D. (2019). Augmented and virtual reality in education: Immersive learning research. *Journal of Educational Computing Research, 57*(7), 1619–1625.

Byron, K. (2008). Carrying too heavy a load? The communication and miscommunication of emotion by email. *Academy of Management Review, 33*(2), 309–327.

Carless, D., Salter, D., Yang, M., & Lam, J. (2011). Developing sustainable feedback practices. *Studies in higher education, 36*(4), 395–407.

Chen, P.-S. D., Gonyea, R., & Kuh, G. (2008). Learning at a distance: Engaged or not? *Innovate: Journal of Online Education, 4*(3), 1–7.

Comer, D. R., & Lenaghan, J. A. (2013). Enhancing discussions in the asynchronous online classroom: The lack of face-to-face interaction does not lessen the lesson. *Journal of Management Education, 37*(2), 261–294.

Conner, J. W., & Chalmers-Neubauer, I. (1989). Mrs. Schuster adopts discussion: A four-week experiment in an English classroom. *English Education, 21*(1), 30–38.

Green, T., Alejandro, J., & Brown, A. H. (2009). The retention of experienced faculty in online distance education programs: Understanding factors that impact their involvement. *International Review of Research in Open and Distance Learning, 10*(3), 1–15.

Hailey Jr., D. E., Grant-Davie, K., & Hult, C. A. (2001). Online education horror stories worthy of Halloween: A short list of problems and solutions in online instruction. *Computers and Composition, 18*(4), 387–397.

Hew, K. F., Cheung, W. S., & Ng, C. S. L. (2010). Student contribution in asynchronous online discussion: A review of the research and empirical exploration. *Instructional Science, 38*(6), 571–606.

Hillman, D. C. A. (1999). A new method for analyzing patterns of interaction. *American Journal of Distance Education, 13*(2), 37–47.

Li, C.-S., & Irby, B. (2008). An overview of online education: Attractiveness, benefits, challenges, concerns and recommendations. *College Student Journal, 42*(2), 1–10.

Palloff, R. M., & Pratt, K. (2011). *The excellent online instructor: Strategies for professional development.* San Francisco: John Wiley & Sons.

Richardson, J. T. E. (1994). Mature students in higher education: academic performance and intellectual ability. *Higher Education, 28*(3), 373–386.

Vonderwell, S., Liang, X., & Alderman, K. (2007). Asynchronous discussions and assessment in online learning. *Journal of Research on Technology in Education, 39*(3), 309–328.

Chapter 9

Working with teaching assistants and other faculty

In this chapter we answer questions about supervising TAs, assuring that they grade fairly, and working with other faculty, including co-teaching.

9.1 How can TAs help me and my online students?

A high-quality learning experience requires that students interact with their faculty, online as well as on-campus. When enrollments grow, it takes faculty more time to interact with their students, and this becomes a limiting factor in educational quality. The usual reason to have TAs in a course is so that there can be more students in it, without unduly compromising the quality of teaching. While early dreams of online education imagined courses with unlimited enrollment, students learning simply and easily from lectures, decades of online experience have shown that this model doesn't work as well as courses where students interact with faculty.

TAs improve enrollment scalability, because they handle routine tasks, such as grading, for faculty. This gives faculty more time to focus on teaching, addressing student concerns about the course, and final grading.

TAs can help you improve your course in many ways, including identifying:

- lecture material that students have trouble understanding;
- assignments that don't challenge students enough;
- assignments that challenge students too much;
- improvements to test questions (or creating new questions); and
- emerging topics that you may not be aware of.

In some online programs, TAs may also help with the implementation of the course. For example, they may take the text faculty have written, copy it into the **LMS**, and format it. They may also set up assignments, quizzes, and tests. One of the most important tasks that TAs can do is to check recently changed or known-to-be-problematic sections of the course. This helps

DOI: 10.4324/9781003161288-9

them learn about the updates to the course, and they may spot technical errors or pedagogical weaknesses. You should ask them to check all updated material before your course opens to students.

As with on-campus courses, TAs are often responsible for grading assignments and answering routine student questions. They may also guide **study groups** and group problem-solving sessions. TAs can attend and grade student presentations, allowing you to have concurrent presentations. TAs are usually in an ideal position to identify struggling students; make sure you ask them to let you know ASAP about anyone they see having trouble. (For more on struggling students, see Chapter 11.)

Because they do most of the assignment grading, TAs can also help you revise assignments and **rubrics**. For example, an assignment may be too large a step beyond what students have already done; TAs may help you modify it so that students are better prepared for it or by suggesting an easier, transitional assignment. TAs can also help you create or update rubrics, because they grade everything and they know the kinds of mistakes that students make. (For more on rubrics, see Appendix G.)

9.2 How do I select, train, mentor, and support my online TAs

TAs typically have primary responsibility for grading assignments, supervising discussions, and answering students' questions. Each of them is usually responsible for a small group of students, for whom they may also conduct **synchronous** question-and-answer sessions. They may also respond to posts in **asynchronous** forums designed for asking faculty questions; this speeds the response, helping students learn. You must carefully choose, train, and manage them, as they usually have no teaching experience.

> Hint: Some programs also have tutors, who may help students formulate their ideas in writing and help with basic mathematics or statistics.

Unfortunately, some schools have been sloppy over the years in selecting and training (or failing to train) their TAs, and tales of disengaged, overworked, and hard-to-understand grad students are common. Fortunately, you can avoid these problems. When you're selecting your TAs, you need to pay close attention to both their knowledge of the subject matter and their ability to communicate with students. We have found that program graduates who helped their classmates when they were students make good candidates.

Even the most promising candidates should be evaluated and trained in the tasks they'll perform as TAs. One approach is to have a candidate TA enrolled in a course under the tutelage of the faculty and other experienced TAs. This approach works well, but it takes a lot of faculty time and it can take one or two terms to complete the training.

A more efficient approach is to have a short online course to train and evaluate them. Our course is two weeks long and candidates act as TAs. We grade them, and about 70 percent do well enough to pass. They'll still need to learn how to grade your particular assignments, and you'll still need to check their grading. You should then continue their training and development while your courses are running; this is important for retaining TAs.

There may be times when a TA isn't performing as well as you expect; common problems are grading too slowly or not providing enough feedback. If this happens, you need to reach out to them, pointing out in detail what they need to do differently and asking them if there is something keeping them from doing their job well that you can help with. In our larger programs we have reserve TAs enrolled in courses, prepared to help with a short-term problem, or even replacing an underperforming TA.

You should communicate with your TAs individually any time there is an issue that you think needs to be addressed. You should meet with your TAs as a group at least once per week, and in these meetings you should cheer them on and ask if they have any questions or concerns. Many faculty find it helpful to prepare a set of slides to go over specific areas where students often have trouble. In some programs, faculty may evaluate their TAs at the end of each course.

9.3 How do I manage the workload distribution across my online TAs?

When setting up your TAs' groups, try to have the same number of students in each. Your LMS may be able to assign students randomly to each group, but if students drop or add the course, your TAs may still wind up with different workloads. This may also occur if a TA has exceptionally high-workload students.

You can level the workload by:

- reassigning students to another TA;
- asking another TA to help the overloaded one, without reassigning students; or
- placing students who add the course late in a lower-workload group.

These techniques can also be used to reduce the workload of a TA who is sick or otherwise unable to do all their work.

9.4 How do I ensure that my online TAs are grading consistently?

Anytime you use TAs your students will wonder if grading is consistent; they may compare their graded assignments. The easiest way to address this is to provide rubrics that specify how the items are to be graded. Sometimes it's necessary for rubrics to include annotated examples of submissions with different grades. (For more on rubrics, see Appendix G.)

When you're unsure if your TAs are grading comparably, check the overall grades to determine whether any one TA's grading is significantly different from the others. If you find discrepancies, you should check the grading that is out of line. TAs will often grade differently when they are first grading something, such as a new assignment, so you should check their work. Whenever you catch inconsistent grading, you should correct it.

> Hint: It's usually enough to compute the average grades for each of the TAs and check if any of them are significantly higher or lower than the others. If there are significant differences, you should look at the scores for each item to see which were graded differently.

9.5 How can I co-teach an online course with other faculty?

Having more than one faculty in a course generally works better online than on campus. Online technologies allow multiple channels of communication, which can be directed at more than one faculty. Sometimes the same section of a course may need more than one faculty to teach it (Graziano & Navarrete, 2012). Common situations are when a:

- faculty member is learning how to teach a course under the tutelage of more experienced faculty;
- course has such high enrollments that one faculty member would be overwhelmed by the workload; and
- course covers disparate areas that are difficult for one faculty member to teach.

One of the safest and most effective ways to train faculty who are new to online is to put them in a course taught by an experienced colleague. It's important that new faculty undertake tasks in all areas, including synchronous sessions, office hours, grading, and handling student issues. When new faculty encounter situations that they are uncomfortable with or don't know how to handle, they can ask their more experienced colleague for help.

If you have a course that needs more than one faculty member to teach it well, you need a way to divide the work, including who'll:

- manage TAs;
- manage announcements and other broadcast communication with students;
- teach synchronous sessions;
- answer student questions;
- return graded assignments, quizzes, and tests; and
- determine the final course grades.

> Hint: When there are multiple faculty, you should make it clear to students who is responsible for answering their questions.

One way to address courses that cover disparate topics is to have different faculty take primary responsibility for each. For example, we offer a course in genealogy in which different faculty teach the subjects in which they are expert. One teaches probate records, while in another **module**, someone else teaches the planning and reporting of genealogical research.

> Hint: If the reason that you're considering having several faculty co-teach a **high-touch** course is because there's high enrollment and you want to maintain an excellent student–faculty ratio, we suggest that you ask your administration to offer the course more often. This provides students more opportunities to take it, and you more opportunities to update it.

9.6 How do I bring in guest lecturers to speak to my online class?

One of the great advantages of teaching online is that you can bring in guest lecturers from anywhere, as long as they have decent internet access. Your guests should be able to use the same **videoconferencing** system as you do. They should normally come later in the course, when your students are prepared to understand what they have to say and ask good questions.

If possible, schedule guest speakers at your regular synchronous session time. Your lecturer and students will benefit from dialogue, so it's best to hold guest lectures synchronously, but depending on the availability of your guests, you may have to record their lectures in advance.

You should always record these sessions anyway, for students who can't attend and for review. Ask your guests for permission to incorporate the recordings in future offerings of the course.

In some courses you may be able to have several guest lecturers covering the same areas. In these situations, you can ask the lecturers the same questions, and then later, you can edit the recordings to create a video that compares and contrasts their views.

References

Graziano, K. J., & Navarrete, L. A. (2012). Co-teaching in a teacher education classroom: Collaboration, compromise, and creativity. *Issues in Teacher Education*, *21*(1), 109–126.

Chapter 10

Addressing online student issues

In this chapter we describe ways in which faculty can interact with their online students and cover the unique challenges of teaching them. We describe ways of giving them feedback and how **synchronous** sessions can foster online student participation and confidence.

10.1 How do I help students make the transition to online?

One of the most effective ways of helping your students make the transition to online is to offer an orientation to the **LMS** and the course website. It should cover how to navigate in the LMS, how to download and upload files, and how to use the discussion boards and other technologies. Students should be given enough time to complete it before a course starts, so that they can concentrate on their course, rather than learning how to use the LMS. If the orientation hasn't been developed, you can conduct an informal session synchronously, sharing the LMS screen and demonstrating how to use it.

We recommend that you conduct a welcoming course introduction synchronous session on the first day of the course, so that your students have a chance to get to know you and what you expect of them. These course introduction sessions are most effective if students can ask questions and share their concerns. This is similar to the first day of a course on campus, except that your students may ask you questions about the LMS and technologies that will be used in the course.

> Hint: Prepare slides for all the points you wish to cover in your introduction, so you don't forget what you wanted to say and so students will have a record of it. This is a good way to start all courses, not just your online ones.

DOI: 10.4324/9781003161288-10

One common student concern when they are new to online is that they may miss something important in a synchronous lecture and not be able to find it again. You can address this by assuring them that all material that is presented synchronously will be recorded and available to them throughout the course.

Some students like to know what is in the course ahead of time. A good way to accommodate this concern is to email students the syllabus, the **study guides**, and, if feasible, the first **module** and early assignments, before the course opens. We recommend that you make the whole course visible from day one, so they can preview what's coming, to plan their time and worry less about what lies ahead.

A classic source of student anxiety, both online and on campus, is how they'll be graded. Be very clear, both in the syllabus and in your course introduction, how you'll grade your students. **Rubrics** make clear how you'll grade their submissions. (For more on rubrics, see Appendix G.) It also helps if you let students know that they can ask you during the term how they are doing in the course. Let your students see their scores in the LMS grade book and show them how to figure out what their likely grade will be.

We suggest that you phone your students during the course, to get a sense of how they're feeling about it. This is a great opportunity to reassure them that if they put enough effort into the course, they'll do fine, and to listen to and alleviate their concerns. It's useful to set up a questionnaire the first day of class to ask your students their phone numbers and the best day and time to call. We have found that if you have students in many time zones, you should also ask for the time zone they're in. Be sure to provide your phone number so they'll recognize it and answer the call!

Your students will have a better time making the transition to online if the course eases them in by building on their classroom experiences. In conventional classrooms they would read books and listen to lectures. **Asynchronous** content will be similar to textbooks; synchronous content will be similar to lectures. Your students will appreciate your covering important concepts in both. For example, you may cover a topic in an asynchronous lecture, and also summarize it and answer questions about it in a synchronous session. The combination of these modes builds students' confidence.

You can also guide your students to use the student support services available at your institution. Academic advisors or student services can help your students make the transition to online by reassuring them, and also by guiding them to other services such as technical support or an online library.

10.2 How can students engage with their faculty online?

In a well-designed online course, students can engage with their faculty in many ways (Henrie et al., 2015). If they engage with faculty, both asynchronously and synchronously, they have a better opportunity to learn the material well. For example, a student may learn most of a topic from asynchronous content, and then ask their faculty questions in a synchronous session on points where they need help or want to learn more.

Students can communicate with their faculty synchronously using **videoconferencing**, phone calls, and even meeting in person, if it's a **blended** course. (For more on blended courses, see Chapter 7.) When you're meeting with your students in a videoconference session, your **engagement** with them will be much better if you can see them. Encourage your students to turn on their webcams and microphones; if videoconferencing with your students is an important part of the course, ask your students to use headsets. If they can't (or won't) turn on their webcams, ask them to upload a photo of themselves to help you and their classmates feel connected. Videoconferencing helps you reassure your students that you're there to clarify and answer questions.

You can engage with your students asynchronously in many ways, both inside and outside the course (Riggs & Linder, 2016). Inside the course, your most common forms of asynchronous communication are usually discussion forums and email, using the LMS. If you want to broadcast to all your students, it may be best to use the LMS announcement tool. Sometimes courses include **wikis**, blogs, or journals; these can be implemented using the LMS, external websites, or apps. (For more on engaging with your students asynchronously with **formative evaluations**, see Appendix E.)

10.3 Is it important for my online students to discuss what they are studying with each other?

Yes.

There are three main reasons why it's important for students to communicate with and learn from each other:

- When students interact with each other, it reassures them that other students in the course are having similar problems. For example, they can share their struggles with the homework, and not feel like they're the only ones in the course who had trouble.
- When students discuss the material and ask each other questions, they practice articulating what they're studying.

- When students can explain the subject matter to each other and answer each other's questions, they improve their mutual understanding.

The larger your course, the more important it is for your students to be able to have informal communications with each other. Such communication is easier in small groups, so you may want to break up the class into groups or encourage them to form their own.

10.4 How do I set online student expectations on grading?

You manage your students' expectations about how they'll be graded just as you would on campus:

- Your syllabus should clearly specify how graded items are weighted.
- Your syllabus should specify submission policies, including any late penalties or resubmission rules.
- Each of your graded items should have an associated rubric which defines the standards against which they are graded (what earns an A, B, etc.). (For more on rubrics, see Appendix G.)
- Consider providing examples of graded work, because they make it clear what you expect; this also discourages **grade begging** and complaints.

Your course introduction lecture should cover grading and you should ask your students if they have any questions about it.

> Hint: You can get examples of outstanding submissions from previous times you've taught the course. You should include the grading marks and comments, obtain permission from students to use their work, and remove their names.

10.5 How many hours per week are online students expected to study?

Unlike on-campus courses, where it's obvious how much time students will spend in class, it's less clear how much time students will spend with their online lectures. Similarly, on-campus students learn that they need to spend several hours outside of class for each hour they spend in the classroom, but that doesn't work online.

The number of hours online students are expected to study depends on the number of required synchronous activity hours and the amount of asynchronous material. All required synchronous time should be counted, such as synchronous sessions, module introductions, review sessions, and group work, such as problem-solving or team meetings.

Online you need to make more of an effort to make sure that students have a way to check in with each other to discuss the workload and amount of time they're studying. Without this, it's easy for a student to feel isolated—"I'm the only one failing"—and drop the course. (For more on creating such an online discussion forum, see Appendix D.)

If you think some students will have difficulty completing work on time, you should build your courses so that students can submit work after the deadline without compromising the integrity of the course. This can be done if solutions are not published to the entire class at the deadline, but rather to individual students after they have submitted an assignment. (For more on **academic integrity**, see Chapter 14.)

10.6 How do I know if my online students are attending class?

It may be important for you to identify students who aren't attending class, because they may be at risk of not learning the material. Some faculty feel strongly enough about this that they take attendance; others, particularly in advanced courses, let students decide whether or not attending synchronous sessions is the best use of their time.

There are different ways to take attendance, in both the asynchronous and synchronous parts of your courses. Methods such as non-anonymous polls, surveys, or formative evaluations work in both modes of teaching. You can also tell when your students last logged into the LMS or videoconferencing system and see how much time each of them spent in the course by viewing the activity or attendance reports, or the server logs. Server logs also allow you to see which students watched recordings of the synchronous sessions.

You can tell how frequently your students attend synchronous sessions and how long they stay. If you're using a videoconferencing system and your students use webcams, you'll be able to see who is logged in and whether or not they are watching. You can also periodically take screen shots of students and use that to take attendance. Even if their cameras are off, the system still lists their names.

> Hint: To see which students signed into class with their cameras off and then walked away, allow the videoconference to go for extra time after the class is over. Students who are still there will know to sign off, but those who abandoned their computers won't.

10.7 How do I encourage my online students to participate in synchronous sessions?

Many of the techniques for encouraging your students to participate in synchronous sessions are the same as in on-campus classrooms (Vu & Fadde, 2013). Ask students questions and encourage them to ask questions, too. Encourage discussions between students. Have slides prepared for topical synchronous sessions.

The most motivating synchronous sessions are when everyone can talk and see each other, so we recommend that everyone use webcams and the best possible audio setup. (See Appendix H for more on audio setups.) If there are too many students in a synchronous session, you should conduct more sessions, to keep the attendance low enough so that everyone can participate.

Students will be drawn into your synchronous discussions if you tell stories and lessons learned from your experience. Your students will be more motivated if your synchronous sessions are interactive and engaging.

> Hint: If you think that a segment of your synchronous session worked very well, consider incorporating it as a video in your asynchronous lecture. Your students' comments may enrich these recordings. If you want to use them, be sure to get permission from each student. Keep it short; unless you have cinematic-quality production and a script to match, stay under ten minutes.

10.8 How do I interact with online students in synchronous sessions?

Synchronous sessions serve many critical roles in online courses, including helping you get to know your students and helping them get to know you. Dialogue is easier in synchronous sessions, so they're particularly effective in helping students overcome difficulties. You should strive to keep your synchronous sessions fairly short to make good use of your students' time and to keep them from losing interest. (For more about running synchronous sessions, see Appendix C.)

When teaching synchronously online you may need to create or show drawings for your students on the fly. This can be done with the screen and slide-sharing features of videoconferencing tools. If you expect to draw equations, formulas, or other things that are not easily entered on a keyboard, we recommend using a **document camera**.

It's important that you manage the audio when you're interacting with your students in synchronous sessions. Common problems are students speaking over you and each other, audio feedback, and background noises that ruin their experience. If you anticipate problems with audio, it's best to start with participants muted. Sometimes you may need to mute an individual student if there is background noise or feedback. We recommend that you ask all of them to use headsets, because they eliminate audio feedback and greatly reduce background noise. (For more on managing audio, see Appendix H.)

10.9 How do I help my online students work in groups?

In higher-enrollment courses, you can divide students into groups to facilitate discussions and student interaction:

- Bring together students who share learning needs ("groups of a feather"). For example, one of the authors had several students in a database course who were wrestling with difficult data warehouse design issues at work, so he put them in the same group.
- Group students according to what they're studying. For example, we have students in the same database management course using different tools, and we place them in groups according to the tools they're using. Similarly, some students in this course are concentrating on health informatics, so we place them together in a group with health-informatics-related assignments.
- Suggest that students who live near each other meet to study and work together.
- Organize groups based on when people are available; this can accommodate students who work nights or are in distant time zones.

Sometimes students will organize their own **study groups**, either in the course or using an external website. If they want to study together, you can help them by creating group **study rooms** in the course, configured so that students can control them. Occasionally it's also helpful for these student-organized groups to have their own discussion forums and a place to exchange files.

Be prepared to supervise the activities in your groups. Students may need help with the subject matter. Or, sometimes one student won't let other students participate enough. When this happens, you'll need to intervene by letting your students know that everyone needs to participate, that students who are reluctant to do so should take courage, and that students who are monopolizing the dialogue should back off.

If you have many groups, monitoring them can take a lot of time. One way to do this efficiently is to schedule periodic group meetings where you can review their work, answer questions, and provide guidance. You can also monitor your groups more easily and frequently by enrolling yourself in the main group discussions. In large courses, you can assign TAs to supervise the groups (for more on working with TAs, see Chapter 9). Making notes will help you grade students' contributions.

Indeed, one of the ongoing challenges in group work is how you determine who made significant contributions to the group and how you grade the individual students. Fortunately, this is easier online, because you can monitor the progress of the groups, attend group meetings, and learn who is making the contributions.

In cooperative group activities, it's normal that one or a few students will come to lead the group, initiating many activities, and dominating the discussions. At times these students may impede other students' learning by discouraging them and effectively preventing them from participating in the dialogues. You can counter this by designing group work rubrics that identify and reward individual contributions as well as leadership contributions. (See Appendix G for more on grading rubrics.)

10.10 How can my online students work on group projects?

Teamwork and communication skills are critical for most jobs, and the best way to learn them is by practicing them in supervised group projects. Online students can meet using videoconferencing and collaborate using websites designed to support group activities, such as sharing documents. Online projects can include distributed work and the coordination of geographically dispersed teams. If you provide your students with the same tools used in business, such as Slack or Microsoft Teams, they'll also benefit from the experience.

One of the main advantages of group projects is that they allow students to work on larger projects than the "toy" projects that they could do by themselves. This will better prepare them for the larger projects and more complex tasks that they'll need to do in their careers. When a group of students is working on a project that involves many skills, they can divide the work and choose what they work on. Sometimes students will want to use the skills that they have already mastered. One of our faculty deals with this by intervening and reassigning students to different tasks.

You can design group projects so that all students need to contribute to tasks associated with key learning objectives.

> Hint: We recommend having a grading rubric that rewards students who help pull reluctant members of their groups into the **learning activities**. (For more on grading rubrics, see Appendix G.)

10.11 How can my students do presentations online?

Your students can do presentations online the same way that you lecture online—using videoconferencing tools. If your class is small enough, and the presentation short enough, then your student can present to you and the entire class. If your class is larger, you should divide your students into groups and have them present at different times, and only require students in a group to attend their classmates' presentations. If you have TAs, then multiple groups can do their presentations at the same time.

These presentations should normally be recorded so that students can review and learn from them. It's often helpful to use recordings of exemplary presentations in later versions of the course, with student permission. It's also useful to have recordings of presentations as evidence in cases of potential academic misconduct, such as if a presentation appears to have been prepared by someone else and the student is unable to answer questions about the content that anyone who prepared it should be able to answer.

> Hint: Provide a videoconferencing room for your students, where they can practice their presentations. They should be able to record and review their sessions.

References

Henrie, C. R., Halverson, L. R., & Graham, C. R. (2015). Measuring student engagement in technology-mediated learning: A review. *Computers & Education*, 90, 36–53.

Riggs, S. A., & Linder, K. E. (2016). Actively engaging students in synchronous online classes. *IDEA Paper No. 64*. IDEA Center, Kansas State University, Manhattan, 1–10.

Vu, P., & Fadde, P. J. (2013). When to talk, when to chat: Student interactions in live virtual classrooms. *Journal of Interactive Online Learning, 12*(2), 41–52.

Chapter 11

Working with online students who may need extra help

In this chapter we answer questions about techniques that motivate students and activities that encourage and guide students online. We discuss how to identify and help students who are falling behind and how faculty can help their students succeed. We also describe how to handle student misconduct in online courses.

11.1 How do I let my online students know that I am available to help them succeed in the course?

Consistent, clear communication is required to assure your students that you care about their success in the course and will help them succeed. You should begin communicating this before the course launches, by emailing your students, providing them with the syllabus, and guiding them on how to prepare for the course. You should also share your contact information and invite your students to reach out to you before the course opens. One of our faculty sends the following announcement to his students before his courses launch:

> Dear Students,
> We want to make sure that you fully understand that our staff and I are fully committed to helping you learn and understand the material and making sure that you can apply it in the workforce.
> We are here to support and guide you. We want you to flourish throughout this course and learn to look at technology, business, and industry from a different perspective.
> We want to give you the spark which helps ignite your curiosity about why business and technology are the way they are, and where they are going.
> If you need help with anything, please ask me or your teaching assistant directly. If you are not going to be able to complete an assignment or

DOI: 10.4324/9781003161288-11

quiz on time, please let us know immediately so we can work with you to complete it.

I want to reassure you, we are here for you, we support you, we are committed to your education and success.

You can reach out to me or your teaching assistant any time!

I will talk to you Tuesday 11/3 in our first live classroom to kick things off! In the meantime, if you need anything please reach out.

Adam Arakelian
Boston University

The syllabus should communicate your care for your students. For example, your late submission policy might state that if students don't submit an assignment on time and they have a good reason, then you won't penalize them. You should let them know that you'll conduct weekly office hours, where students can ask you any question about the course, and that you'll meet with them individually if they request it.

Emphasize in the course introduction video or **synchronous** session that you measure your success by your students' success. As the course is running and your students see that you really are willing to meet with them in **videoconferencing** sessions or speak with them on the phone if they need help, they'll become confident in your support.

Synchronous sessions will also help you communicate your care for your students; this works best if they can talk with you and ask you questions. The most effective sessions are ones where faculty and students are relaxed, joking, and laughing.

11.2 How do I motivate my online students to study and learn?

You lay the foundation for your students' motivation when you're developing a course (Johnson & Aragon, 2003). If your students want to learn what you're teaching, they'll begin with good motivation, and your job is to sustain it. If they don't yet know that they'll benefit from what you're teaching, then you'll need to use the techniques covered in the rest of this section.

You can begin motivating your students with emails you send out before the course launches. Start the emails by welcoming your students and letting them know that you care about their success in the course. The focus of your emails should be helping them prepare for the course. The syllabus and early assignments will help with that, as well as your availability to answer their questions. Tell your students that the course has been designed to challenge them and that they'll develop skills in their study that will help them in their academic life and beyond.

Students don't like busywork or content that is off-topic; keep your course content as concise as feasible, and focused on the learning objectives (Hanstedt, 2018). Students value how well you respect their study time, so your asynchronous content should be clear, and any videos should be short. Your assignments should be clearly relevant, giving students an opportunity to practice what they've just studied; ideally, they should also be fun.

One way to motivate your students is by meeting their learning needs in the ways that work best for them. Because students learn in different ways, it helps to present the content in different ways. For example, you can include recordings of your on-campus lectures in an asynchronous course for students who learn best by listening. You'll have students with different preparation and learning skills and goals, so it's best to add both remedial and advanced topics to your asynchronous content: Weaker students will feel motivated by the extra support, while more advanced students will feel motivated by the more challenging material.

Competition can also be a great motivator. If students can see where their scores fall in the class distribution, it will inspire some to try to beat their classmates.

When you teach a course, you should reassure your students that you'll help them succeed in it:

- Make an effort to get to know your students by learning their names.
- Be approachable and remind them of your office hours.
- Encourage your students to form **study groups** and create synchronous rooms for them.
- Record all synchronous sessions; this reduces student anxiety and increases their motivation, because they know that they can review them later.
- Conduct videoconference group office hours at scheduled times, and also for individual students.
- Phone your students, ask them how they are doing, and offer to help. We have found that they love it.
- In advanced courses, help your students study material that goes beyond that in the syllabus.

11.3 How do I get my online students interested in learning what I am teaching?

No matter what course you teach, online or not, if you want to make your teaching successful, you need to interact enthusiastically with your students. The best faculty always try to instill in their students a love for the subject matter, and your students will be more interested in what you teach if they see that you're passionate about the material and its applications. One of the authors inspires his students by illustrating his lectures with accounts of consulting and problems he's solved.

Show that you're looking forward to them learning the material well enough that you can work with them in applying it. For example, if you teach a forestry course and cover the identification of trees, you could say that you look forward to everyone walking through the woods near them and sharing pictures of invasive species with their cell phones. Similarly, if you teach a creative writing course, you can spend some time on the practical side of publishing, like showing the students how to write a query letter.

Your students will be interested in what you teach if you show them how what they are learning will be useful in their careers and lives. You can foster this by providing examples and assignments that are manifestly practical. For example, if you teach series in a math class, you can show how it's used to calculate compound interest. Similarly, if you teach the psychology of relationships, you can show how this applies to their own lives.

One of the keys to capturing your students' attention is adapting your presentation to their interests. For example, if you teach a social science course during a time of societal change, you can use it to illustrate points in your lectures, and your students will be drawn in. One of the authors used this method in a management course during the burgeoning competition between Amazon and Walmart. He used this strategic competition as a case study threading through the entire course; the students found articles on this competition in the news and posted links for the class.

11.4 How can I help my online students feel more connected and less isolated?

When online students feel connected with the course content, faculty, and each other, it improves their learning and the likelihood that they'll complete the course (Beaudoin, 2002). In many courses, group assignments can help students learn skills such as cooperative problem-solving, and also help them connect with their classmates. Many students, particularly those new to online courses, benefit from activities that help them get to know each other, share ideas, collaborate, and lead discussions (Conrad & Donaldson, 2011).

You can do many things to foster connections, including:

- In high-enrollment courses, organize your students into groups that are small enough so that they can get to know each other.
- Encourage your students to form study groups, by creating **study rooms** and by offering to drop in (or have your TAs do so) if they wish.

- Encourage students to link to one another through appropriate social media, such as LinkedIn, or professional organizations.
- Include a separate column in the grade book for class contributions. Give students credit for contributions that help their classmates learn. You should have a **rubric** for this. (For more on this, see Appendix G.)
- Create an "introduce yourself" asynchronous discussion forum, where students can describe themselves, and post pictures and videos of themselves. There should be a forum for each group.
- Create asynchronous discussion forums to build a sense of community, such as an ungraded, "watercooler" discussion forum where students can talk about anything they want.
- Have synchronous sessions where your students can talk with you and each other. On campus, students often chat before and after class; your students can do this online if you open your synchronous sessions early and keep them open for a while after you're done. (See Chapter 14 for how to encourage students to turn on their webcams and Appendix H on successful audio.)

11.5 Are there any special considerations when teaching adult students online?

Adult students are usually more mature, have more experience, and are more motivated than traditional undergraduates, and this makes them easier to teach. However, adult students usually have work, family, and other responsibilities, so we need to help them meet these responsibilities while they study (Polson, 1993). Their ability to continue in the course can depend on you making good use of their time and being flexible; this has a huge effect on student retention.

Adult students usually know why they are taking a course or program. They may need a degree, a certificate, or knowledge to advance their careers, or they may simply want to learn. Adult students may be less tolerant of time spent on tangential material, so you should be careful to make good use of their time and not wander off the learning objectives of the course (Knowles, Holton III, & Swanson, 2014). Make the value of the assignments clear to your adult students (Kenner & Weinerman, 2011). If you're not sure what your adult students want to learn, ask them. They'll tell you and be grateful if you cover what you didn't know they needed. You can also use this as guidance when you update the course.

Another special consideration when teaching adult students is that they have many demands on their time and some of them may be more important than their studies (Doherty, 2012). Many adult students have children or other relatives who need their care and attention, while others have serious professional responsibilities that cannot be ignored or deferred—and some have both. Fortunately, following best practices for online teaching should address their concerns:

- Always record your synchronous activities so that students who can't attend can watch the recording. (For more on synchronous activities, see Appendix C.)
- Be flexible; if students don't deliver something on time, and they give you a good reason, give them more time.
- Conduct office hours on weekends in two widely separated times, so that busy students can attend at least one of them. Adult students may have time to study at certain times during the week and not others.
- If you have deliverables that are due on a particular date, make sure your students have had enough time, preferably a whole week, to work on them.

Adult students have more life and work experience, and this should have helped them grow emotionally and intellectually; their maturity may allow faculty to cover more material, more rigorously. Indeed, faculty should be careful not to have learning activities that adult students regard as too low level. Adults have often learned to overcome serious difficulties, so they won't freak out if they are presented with difficult problems to solve, as long as you make it clear that you'll be there to help them if they ask.

11.6 How can I help online students who need prerequisite or advanced material?

You'll inevitably encounter students in your online courses who are either underprepared or overprepared.

Sometimes students need help before starting a program, particularly if they're changing to a new field, or returning after a long absence; you'll be able to tell from their admissions applications. Some graduate programs have **transition courses** to cover this sort of thing, offering the essential prerequisite material currently being taught to undergraduates. For example, students in a graduate management program who lack preparation in mathematics, may be required to take a statistics course for managers.

Underpreparation can also be caused by any of the following, alone or in combination:

- students forgetting prerequisite material, because they studied it long ago;
- students not doing well in prerequisite courses;
- students overestimating their preparation; or
- prior coursework not covering the necessary prerequisite material.

You can prevent this from occurring by having your students take a readiness **assessment** before the course launches. If it identifies seriously underprepared students, you can counsel them to transfer to a course for which they are better prepared. You can also build remedial material into the course. Some can be done as **asynchronous** content and some is best provided synchronously, tailored to the students' needs.

You can provide asynchronous content to help these students by:

- distributing readings that cover the prerequisite material before the course launches;
- creating a prerequisite review **Module 0** (For more on this, see Appendix B.);
- supplementing your written lectures with prerequisite material, that can be added as sidebars, popups, or links; or
- creating a glossary that includes terms they may not know.

> Hint: If many students need help with the same topic, consider creating a discussion forum for them.

When you're teaching the course, you may identify students who need additional preparation in specific areas. If students find an assignment too difficult even to start, you can give them a bridging assignment that they are able to complete, to help them finish the original assignment (this can happen early in courses, if it turns out that the prerequisite courses didn't cover material you'd expected). If many students appear to have the same needs, it often works well to conduct a topical synchronous session and let these students know that they need to attend. If only one or two students need help on a topic, it's best to invite them to your office hours. Or, if you have TAs, you can ask them to help these students.

> Hint: You can embed bridging activities in your assignments, saving you effort while the course runs and saving your students the time it takes to ask for help.

You'll probably also encounter students who are operating at a more advanced level than most of the others. This can happen because they have extensive experience or have been studying the subject matter. Sometimes students are taking a course because they need a degree, but they've already mastered much of the material. Sometimes students will want to study more advanced material because they need it for their work or career goals.

In advanced courses, this may occur frequently, and you can prepare for it by:

- adding supplemental advanced material to your written lectures;
- creating alternative assignments that cover advanced material;
- creating advanced topical discussion forums; and
- creating advanced projects that are worth extra credit.

> Hint: You needn't be concerned if truly advanced students earn extra credit, because it won't affect their grades—they're going to get A's anyway.

11.7 How do I identify struggling online students?

When students have trouble in online courses, it's important to identify them as quickly as possible, to help them before they fall further behind. You should make it clear that you want your students to reach out to you if they're having difficulty with any part of the course. Sometimes they will; they may ask you for more time to complete a graded item or contact you to say that they are having trouble understanding a topic or completing an assignment. Sometimes, though, they'll suffer in silence.

On campus, faculty can often tell when students are having difficulty by their facial expressions and body language, such as pained looks or shrugged shoulders. You can sometimes tell from how a student speaks, such as sounding hesitant. Deciphering expressions is more difficult online, and it's impossible if your students don't use webcams.

While it's more difficult to actually see if students are struggling online than in person, there are some tells. The first sign may be when they aren't participating enough in discussions or synchronous sessions (though they might just be shy). Perhaps the most obvious indication is by the nature of their participation, when the questions they ask demonstrate a lack of understanding. It's critical that you encourage your students to ask "dumb" questions, both because it helps you identify students who need help and because it helps you know when you need to cover a topic again in a different way.

When a course is first developed, faculty may not foresee where their students will have problems with the material. We recommend that you keep a record of these topics as they become apparent, and address them by improving the asynchronous content and expanding its **formative evaluation** coverage (Peterson, 2016).

We also recommend that you design your courses with at least one kind of assessment per topic or **module** which is automatically graded or graded promptly, so that students get feedback quickly. Distribute the assessments throughout the module, rather than having them all due on the same day, because this lets both you and your students know they're having problems as soon as possible, while it's easier to recover. For example, discussions may take place on the third day, with an assignment due on the fifth and a quiz on the seventh.

There are several techniques that can help you see how your students are doing:

- Ask many questions, as you would on campus, in synchronous online sessions.
- Require that students attend at least some synchronous sessions, so you can get to know them and monitor how they are doing.
- Check the online activity reports in your **LMS** to see if students have spent too little time in the course to do well.
- Use formative evaluations to identify students who need extra help, even before you see their first quizzes and assignments. This is a great reason to add them to your asynchronous lectures! (For more on formative evaluations, see Appendix E.)
- Keep an eye on late submissions. Sometimes a strong student may just have had an unavoidable delay, but other times late work can be a sign that a student is having trouble keeping up. Make sure that your discussion posts and other graded items have clear deadlines, to give you early warning if students miss them.
- Look out for assignments that seem rushed, or are unfinished.
- Use information from the LMS grade book to identify students who seem to be having difficulty. Some LMSs support tools that will flag these students for you.
- Make use of your TAs, if you have them; they should be aware if their students are having trouble with the material or are struggling to complete the work on time. You should have regular meetings with your TAs to discuss these students and how to help them. (For more on working with TAs, see Chapter 9.)

11.8 How do I help struggling online students?

Once you've determined that students are having difficulty, such as lack of preparation, ineffective studying skills, or language impairments (Sayer et al., 2002), you should reach out to them, reassure them, and ask how you can help. Show that you genuinely want to help them succeed.

Initially, you need to get in touch with the student to schedule a private synchronous session, such as a phone call or private videoconference. Student problems usually fall into one or more of the following areas (Table 11.1).

Table 11.1 Common problem areas for struggling students and what we recommend

Lack of preparation	Identify the areas where they need help. If it's lack of preparation, and you have a Module 0, direct them to the appropriate place in it. (For more on this, see Appendix B.)
Lack of understanding in spite of study	Identify the areas where they need help. If it's easy, tutor them on the spot. If not, arrange for them to do remedial work or get tutoring in those areas.
Inadequate study time or skills	Ask them how many hours a week they study, how they study, and if they study at the best time for them. Tell them how much you expect them to study each week, and the most effective ways for most students to study. Encourage them to study every day, rather than cramming.
Unable to complete assignments on time	Try to tell whether it's a short-term issue, such an illness, or a chronic issue, such as procrastination. If it's a short-term issue, offer them more time. If it's a chronic issue, see the answer in this table for inadequate study time or skills, because an extension will not resolve the problem and they may miss the new deadlines.
An issue with a TA or another student	Discuss the problem with the student and, if appropriate, with the TA or other student. The cause might be a simple temperament conflict or a sign of something more complex.
Personal issues such as illness, trouble at work, or with family	Try to determine if the problem is something you should try to help the student handle or if it requires professional help. Sometimes it's appropriate for you to suggest that they take an **incomplete** to finish the course later. Sometimes, they may want to retake the course.

You should include a lateness policy in your syllabus, which you may later waive. We haven't found it helpful to penalize students for late or incomplete submissions; if something bad has happened to make them late, they're already at a disadvantage, and the penalty puts them at greater risk of failing the course.

Tell your students that even if they can only complete a portion of an assignment, that they should complete what they can, and submit it. Then at least they'll learn what they can from the assignment, and not fall as far behind. If the student explains what prevented them from finishing, you (or your TAs) can help them more effectively. We recommend that you grade students based on the submitted portion, permit them to resubmit when they have completed the work, and earn that grade.

When you're developing your course, you can also incorporate links to tutorial services or writing labs, which can be particularly helpful for students with language impairments. These services typically provide students with help on basic mathematics, writing, and other foundational skills. Tutors are careful not to do the work for the students, but to help them in areas of weakness. If you're concerned that one may have overstepped and actually done the work, you can ask that tutor for a report on exactly what they did to help your students.

11.9 How do I handle overly assertive or aggressive online students?

Sometimes a student can be so assertive in a discussion that it discourages their classmates from participating. You need to deal with overly assertive and aggressive behavior because it can undermine other students' willingness to honestly present their views.

In synchronous sessions, a student might speak over their classmates, disparage their contributions, or not shut up and give them a chance to participate. It can also happen in asynchronous sessions, if a student's posts criticize their classmates or their posts.

There is another kind of student behavior, that while not aggressive or too assertive, can nonetheless interfere with learning. If a student posts frequently in ways that close discussions, it can prevent their classmates from having good opportunities to contribute. You can deal with this by having your syllabus include a discussion rubric that rewards posts that foster good discussion. (For more on this, see Appendix G.)

> Hint: If you create open-ended asynchronous discussion questions, they'll be hard for students to close. You can also create several questions for each topic or create reserve questions that are hidden from students until the original questions have been answered. (You can authorize your TAs to reveal them.)

11.10 How do I handle online student misconduct?

Students can act in ways that interfere with their classmates' learning online, just as they do on campus. Some students are more prone to this kind of misconduct online, because the social distance is greater. They can fail to realize how much they affect others, or even that they are doing so (Hailey Jr., Grant-Davie, & Hult, 2001).

Your institution probably has policies covering this, with procedures for addressing serious student misconduct. You should address student behavior in your syllabus, by referring to your institution's policies and, if necessary, stating that you won't tolerate behavior that undermines learning. You should also address this in your discussion grading rubrics and introductory lecture. (For more on rubrics, see Appendix G.)

Your first course of action should be to confront the aggressive student, explaining why what they did was unacceptable, and referring them to the policy in the syllabus. If they misbehave in a synchronous session, you need to confront them during the session; remember that you should model appropriate behavior by confronting them in a courteous and professional fashion. If the misbehavior is in an asynchronous activity, such as a discussion or email, you should usually ask them to join you in a private synchronous session where you explain what was unacceptable and how they should communicate in your course.

Students usually respond to these confrontations by apologizing and at least attempting to correct their behavior. If a student persists, you should discuss this with whomever in your institution deals with student misconduct, such as a dean of students; they may know of any prior serious misbehavior by the student and will, in any event, be well versed in how to address it. Most institutions have a policy that faculty should not penalize students for misconduct by themselves; this often requires approval by a dean or a hearing before a student conduct committee.

References

Beaudoin, M. F. (2002). Learning or lurking? Tracking the "invisible" online student. *The Internet and Higher Education, 5*, 147–155.

Conrad, R.-M., & Donaldson, J. A. (2011). *Engaging the online learner: Activities and resources for creative instruction*. San Francisco: Jossey-Bass.

Doherty, B. (2012). Tips for teaching adult students. *North American Colleges and Teachers of Agriculture Journal, 56*(1), 1–2.

Hailey Jr., D. E., Grant-Davie, K., & Hult, C. A. (2001). Online education horror stories worthy of Halloween: A short list of problems and solutions in online instruction. *Computers and Composition, 18*(4), 387–397.

Hanstedt, P. (2018). *Creating wicked students: Designing courses for a complex world*. Stylus Publishing, LLC.

Johnson, S. D., & Aragon, S. R. (2003). An instructional strategy framework for online learning environments. *New Directions for Adult and Continuing Education, 100*, 31–43.

Kenner, C., & Weinerman, J. (2011). Adult learning theory: Applications to non-traditional college students. *Journal of College Reading and Learning, 42*(2), 87–96.

Knowles, M. S., Holton III, E. F., & Swanson, R. A. (2014). *The adult learner: The definitive classic in adult education and human resource development* (8th ed.). New York: Routledge.

Peterson, J. L. (2016). Formative evaluations in online classes. *Journal of Educators Online, 13*(1), 1–24.

Polson, C. J. (1993). Teaching Adult Students. *IDEA Paper No. 29.* Center for Faculty Evaluation and Development, Kansas State University, Manhattan, 2–7.

Sayer, M., Chaput De Saintonge, M., Evans, D., & Wood, D. (2002). Support for students with academic difficulties. *Medical Education, 36,* 643–650.

Chapter 12

Getting help for online students with nonacademic issues

Students can face many kinds of challenges that interfere with their studies, from natural disasters to family crises. In this chapter we describe how faculty can recognize these issues and help their students.

For decades, online education has provided a flexible option for many students. During the pandemic, its use by colleges and universities for all students has shown that it's a doable—and reasonable—accommodation for students with disabilities or other issues (Morris & Anthes, 2021). We expect that it will continue to be a valuable tool to help students and retention in the future.

12.1 How do I get help for my online students on nonacademic issues?

Students have lives, and many things can happen that interfere with their studies. We've encountered a wide range of these issues, from having many students without power or internet after Hurricane Katrina to a student's barracks being blown up in Afghanistan, along with his computer and textbooks. Some issues may be personal for students, so you need to deal with them sensitively and may need to consult professionals. Often the best thing for faculty to do is simply to talk with the student, giving them plenty of opportunity to explain what's going on and how they feel.

The most common nonacademic issues that students confront are technical problems having to do with their systems or their ability to use them. (For more on technical issues, see Chapter 13.) Some of these problems are due to natural events that interrupt students' work environment, internet, or power. If only a few students are seriously affected, the best way to handle the situation may be to give them more time to complete their work, by extending the deadlines; if this isn't enough, you can use your institution's **incomplete** policies and procedures. If many students are involved, as has happened during California's blackouts, you may consider holding special **synchronous** sessions to help those students catch up.

DOI: 10.4324/9781003161288-12

Students also encounter work, family, or personal crises that can interfere with their study. You should address this in your syllabus, where you let students know that if something is preventing them from studying, there are things that you can do to help them with the course.

You may also make it clear in your introductory lecture that you recognize that many things can happen and that you can be flexible on academic deadlines, waive penalties for late submissions, and give them additional time after the end of the term to finish their work. Some of these issues may involve private student information, so you should consult your institution's policies on how to handle sensitive student situations. You should also know who to contact for mental and other student health issues.

12.2 How do I get help for online students with emotional or behavioral challenges?

Students can experience a variety of emotional and behavioral problems, and faculty may need help handling them. Dealing with these issues often requires clinical expertise. You should contact administrators in your institution skilled in handling student misbehavior if you suspect that one of your students is struggling or misbehaving because of an emotional or mental health issue. If the behavior suggests that the student may harm themselves or someone else, you should contact your administrators immediately.

If one of your students misbehaves, you should try to understand the situation before acting on it. If the misbehavior is reported in posts or emails, or recorded in synchronous sessions, you need to make sure you see it for yourself. We have found that students will usually correct their behavior if you explain that it's inappropriate and provide guidance on alternatives. One way to discuss this with them is to explain how their behavior affects other students. If the student doesn't respond in a satisfactory manner, you should contact your administration.

12.3 How can I help my online students who are not fluent in the language of instruction?

Many online programs attract students with diverse language backgrounds, and some students may not be fluent in the language of instruction (Eskey & Grabe, 1988). Faculty can do many things to help them, including:

- providing closed captions and transcripts for synchronous sessions;
- avoiding colloquialisms, slang, and uncommon words and phrases;
- creating a glossary; and
- providing language and writing tutors.

These accommodations can help all of your students, not just those who are learning the language. Closed captions, transcripts, and other elements of **universal design** will help hearing-impaired students and those who prefer to read rather than watch a video. (For more on improving your course with universal design, see Chapter 5.) When you're writing your lectures and other **asynchronous** content, try to imagine that the reader is someone who learned the language of instruction in a second-language course; avoid jargon and idioms that are wicked regional.

If you include a glossary, you should consider putting the first usage of each term in a consistent typographical format, so that readers know to look for it. You can even make the term click-sensitive, so it displays the definition.

Students often struggle when they're asked to write essays or reports, in any language; your institution or program can provide tutoring services linked from your course to help them. This works better online than on-campus, because they're easier to access and some services are available 24 hours a day. These may be helpful to students who are learning the language and also to those who are fluent in the language, but have difficulty writing.

12.4 How can I help less-privileged students succeed online?

One of the most important things an educational institution can do to improve the diversity of its student body is to support students with limited financial resources. As online faculty, you can help support these students by recognizing and being sensitive to their situation, and building your online offerings accordingly.

Students with limited financial resources face many problems online simply because they can't afford more recent and expensive computers or higher-quality internet connections. This particularly affects them in synchronous sessions. The fundamental way you can help these students is to make certain that all of the important content is covered in your textbook or asynchronous lectures, and that they can download those lectures for off-line study.

All of your students will benefit if the key material in your course is covered in the asynchronous content and it's designed to be easy for them to download and print, if they need to. This is particularly important for less-privileged students who may have slow or unreliable internet or power, but it also benefits any of your students who may not have access to the internet while traveling.

Some students' living situations may not be conducive to study. For example, they may share a small apartment with their family. The best way to help these students is to make it easier for them to study asynchronously, and take their exams someplace other than at their homes. They'll also benefit if you're flexible in your scheduling of activities and deliverables, so they can study whenever and wherever possible.

Table 12.1 lists common problems faced by less-privileged students and things that you can do to help.

Table 12.1 Problems faced by less-privileged students and how to help them

Problems students may face	Solution(s)
Old, slow computers	• Build your courses so students don't need newer computers—minimize use of resource-heavy media
Slow/no internet at home	• Design the course so that synchronous communication isn't essential to do well • Use **videoconferencing** software that degrades gracefully on slow or unreliable networks
Unreliable internet or power at home	• Design the course so that synchronous communication isn't essential to do well • Schedule synchronous sessions so students can attend from work or elsewhere • Arrange that students can take exams at local libraries, coffee shops, or anywhere with good Wi-Fi
Difficulty affording textbooks	• Tell students which textbooks to buy early, so they can buy used books • If there is a new edition, also support the prior edition • Work with your librarians to put texts on digital reserve
Students who forget material because they need to take financial breaks between courses	• Integrate review material in the course • Email your students well before the term with the syllabus, review material, and guidance on how to prepare
Students who can't study at home	• Don't require your students to speak in synchronous sessions if they're in a place where they have to be quiet, such as a library or next to a sleeping child. Let them use chat • Schedule synchronous sessions so students can attend from work or elsewhere • Arrange that students can study and take exams at local libraries, coffee shops, or anywhere with good Wi-Fi

12.5 How can I accommodate online students from significantly different time zones, countries, and cultures?

Cultural differences can affect your students' understanding of things like intellectual property. Some cultural differences can cause students to get in serious trouble when they are held to ethical standards that they don't know. The most common example is when students from cultures that do not have an old tradition of intellectual property use material written by other people. In some cultures, copying someone else's words or images is regarded as helping a fellow student, but in most European cultures, copying works of music or writing has long been regarded as comparable to theft (Ison, 2018). This cultural disconnect often causes plagiarism problems for faculty and naïve students.

You can prevent these problems by making your program's plagiarism policies clear in your syllabus, and by covering them in your introductory lecture. (For more on fostering **academic integrity**, see Chapter 14.) In some programs with many foreign students, it has proven worthwhile to require them to complete a short online introduction to the culture of the country of instruction.

You also need to be aware that holidays and religious holy days differ widely from country to country, to prevent scheduling conflicts with synchronous events, exams, or major deliverables. You can avoid most of these issues simply by recording your synchronous sessions and being flexible. For example, if a student tells you that they have an important national holiday on a particular date, they can submit their work one day later.

If you teach students who are in many places, allow for time differences, so as not to force distant students to get up in the middle of the night to attend your synchronous sessions. You can address this by scheduling each synchronous session twice, separated by at least eight hours, so that your students can choose a session when they are awake. This will also help students who are night owls and give students having difficulty an opportunity to attend the sessions twice, if they want.

12.6 How can I accommodate online students with disabilities?

There are many kinds of disabilities, and many ways to accommodate them. Your institution has legally mandated policies and procedures for students with disabilities, which you should learn.

Because disability accommodations are required by law in many countries, and because the design of disability accommodations requires specialized skills, most institutions require that students with disabilities contact the institution's Office of Disability and Access Services before they begin their studies.

Disability accommodations require review of students' conditions by medical professionals and design of accommodations by specialists. This process can take weeks, so it should be started as soon as a student is admitted. Your institution may not allow disability accommodations without this approval; when in doubt, contact them.

Sometimes students think they'll do just fine without disclosing their disabilities, but then they find themselves in need of accommodation midway through a course, so they disclose to their faculty. If this happens, you should contact your Office of Disability and Access Services immediately and ask for guidance.

You should design your courses to accommodate students with the most common disabilities. The most common accommodation is allowing students with disabilities extra time for tests. Students with visual disabilities may require modifications to the course content to support **screen readers** or Braille readers. Students with auditory disabilities may require closed captioning of videos and synchronous sessions. Specialists, such as sign language interpreters or **CART** transcriptionists, may need to be scheduled for your synchronous sessions.

If you teach a course that has a student with a disability, you'll need to learn how to work with any assistants and special software that the student uses. Students who have been living with disabilities may tell you what they need from you.

> Hint: It's good practice to record every synchronous session for students to review. It will be especially useful for students with disabilities.

The principles of universal design will guide you in creating courses that work well for everyone. (For more on universal design, see Chapter 5.) The WCAG (Web Content **Accessibility** Guidelines) standards < www.w3.org/TR/WCAG21/> specify how your course website should be constructed so that it will support screen readers and other tools used by students with disabilities.

References

Eskey, D. E., & Grabe, W. (1988). Interactive models for second language reading: Perspectives on instruction. In P. Carrel, J. Devine, & D. Eskey (Eds.), *Interactive Approaches to Second Language Reading*. New York: Cambridge University Press.

Ison, D. C. (2018). An empirical analysis of differences in plagiarism among world cultures. *Journal of Higher Education Policy and Management*, 40(4), 291–304.

Morris, A., & Anthes, E. (2021). For Some College Students, Remote Learning Is a Game Changer. *The New York Times* www.nytimes.com/2021/08/23/health/covid-college-disabilities-students.html.

Chapter 13

Resolving technical problems in online courses

While technology enables online education, it can fail or frustrate us as well. In this chapter we describe common technical problems and how faculty can deal with them.

13.1 How can online faculty and students get technical support?

You need to know how you and your students get technical support for your course. It may be by telephone, email, or web form. Because different skills are needed to solve different kinds of technical problems, different people may provide different kinds of technical support. For example, your institution may have **instructional designers** handle support for the **LMS**, and the IT department handle problems with student and faculty computers. You'll get a problem resolved more quickly if you send it to the right people.

> Hint: Once you know who your students should contact to submit technical support issues, you should put that information in the course, either in the syllabus or in a special "Help" section, if there is one.

Some technical problems, such as slow server response or server outages, aren't usually handled by faculty or instructional designers, but by your institution's IT staff. Again, be sure you know who these people are and how to contact them. (For more on what to do when technology isn't working during class, see Appendix I.)

DOI: 10.4324/9781003161288-13

13.2 How do I troubleshoot online technical issues?

Some students will ask you for help with technical issues, rather than the IT staff, and you'll need to be ready. Some problems arise because students don't understand how to use the LMS or **add-ons**. Over time you'll gain enough experience with the LMS and other teaching tools to quickly help these students, but early in your online teaching, it'll be helpful if you have someone in the course with you with more experience, to whom you can refer students who ask questions that you don't know how to answer.

The first step in solving a technical issue is getting an accurate description of the problem. If you can show the problem with a screenshot, it'll save a lot of time and miscommunication, particularly if you need to refer the problem to someone else. Ask for a screenshot of the student's complete screen, including the address bar of their browser. This'll show you what they're seeing and let you verify that they're using the correct program and are on the right page. You'd be surprised how many times students aren't on the right page. No wonder they can't find what they're looking for!

The second step in solving a technical problem is figuring out if the problem is with the student's computer, the network, or with your course. If you go to the same page, do you have the same problem? If so, the problem is probably with the course. You or instructional designers can easily correct many of the minor technical problems in your course, such as broken or misdirected links. Are all students having the problem or only one of them?

> Hint: If everyone has the same problem, then the problem is with the course. If only one student has a problem, the issue is not with the course.

If you can't reproduce the problem on your computer, then it's probably on the student's end. Next, isolate variables to narrow down where the problem lies. Have them try a different browser and see if that works. If it does, then the problem is with the first browser. If that doesn't work, then the problem might be with their computer or network. Can they open another web page with their browser? If not, then the problem is probably with their network. You can have them contact technical support or their internet service provider.

If the student's problem is that the course is running slowly, and it's not running slowly for you, the cause is probably their network connection or their computer. If other operations on the student's computer run quickly, the problem is probably on the student's network. Ask the student to do something that makes heavy use of their network, such as download a movie, to see if this is really the problem. Network slowness is often transient, because of varying network load, so the problem may go away and recur. You should ask the student whether other people may be making heavy use of the network connection, like housemates watching videos. (For more on what to do when some technology isn't working, see Appendix I.)

13.3 How can I prevent audio problems such as feedback and noise?

You've probably been in a **videoconferencing** session where you've heard loud echoes or noises that disrupted the meeting. Common sources of noise are keyboard clicks or the crackling of snack wrappers near the microphone. If the source of a noise is close to the microphone, it will sound much louder than if it is further away; even the mere rustling of papers near a mic can drown out speech.

The source of noise may also be acoustic feedback, which is caused when someone has enabled both an ordinary microphone and speaker at the same time. The sound from the speaker is picked up by the microphone, where it's sent to the videoconferencing system, which, in turn, sends it back to the speaker, creating a feedback loop.

The most common cause of feedback is when a student uses the built-in microphone and speaker on their computer. This can be prevented if everyone uses headsets, which are designed so that sound from the earpieces isn't picked up by the microphone. You can also prevent feedback by using headphones or earbuds.

> Hint: We recommend that you require your students to use headsets. They needn't be expensive.

When you teach **synchronous** sessions, you may encounter situations where a student's setup is causing feedback. The videoconferencing system should tell you which students are speaking, for example, by putting a colored frame around their picture. If you hear feedback, one of them is causing it, and you can mute their microphones in your videoconferencing system. Once you explain what causes it and how to prevent it, students who you muted will understand, and they can usually fix the problem—they may just need to move the bag of potato chips further away from the mic. (For more on managing audio, see Appendix H.)

13.4 What do I do when a student can't see something in my online course?

A number of technical problems can prevent students from being able to see or hear parts of your course. This happens most commonly because a student is trying to use a browser that is not supported by your course or program. All browsers support HTML, but they differ widely in their support for objects embedded in HTML pages. The browsers that are supported should be listed in your courses.

Table 13.1 Troubleshooting an item that isn't rendering on a web page

Step	Process	Result
Verify that there is a technical problem.	Ask the student to send you a screenshot of their entire window, including the browser address bar.	This will help you verify that the student is doing something reasonable to display the object, including using an approved browser and viewing the correct page.
Verify that the issue isn't with the browser.	Try to open the object in a different browser.	If the object can be rendered in another browser, tell the student to use the browser that works for you.
Verify that the HTML link to the file is syntactically correct.	Validate the HTML, by checking it at <validator.w3.org>	If the page doesn't validate, correct and test again.
Verify that linked files are where you think they should be.	Check that the HTML file and all items linked to it are where you think they should be. (If you need help from an instructional designer to do this, don't be shy about asking.)	If files aren't there, add the file where it should be or correct the link to the file location. (This typically happens when a course is developed on a personal computer and not all the files are moved to the LMS.)
If your object requires helper applications, such as JavaScript, ensure they are linked properly and working.	Find another page that uses the same helper applications and add your object to it. If it works, check the links to the helper applications on the troublesome page.	If your object still doesn't work, it may be defective; see the next step.
Verify that the browser is capable of rendering the object.	Drag and drop the object onto a blank browser window.	If it displays, the problem is probably how it's linked to the page. If it doesn't display, it may be defective or in a format the browser doesn't understand.

When a student can't see something in the course, it should be addressed, no matter what the cause is. Table 13.1 will help you learn what to do when students report that they can't see something in your course.

Chapter 14

Promoting academic integrity in online courses

This chapter addresses questions about **academic integrity**, including how to detect cheating and make it more difficult, for both assignments and tests. We also describe ways to proctor tests online.

14.1 What's the best way to use a grade book for online students?

The **LMS** grade book is more important online than on-campus, because it's more difficult for online students to come up to you before or after class and ask how they're doing. Becoming familiar with your grade book will save you time and improve grading, because it:

- allows you to link graded items so you don't have to enter scores twice;
- calculates your students' grades for you;
- allows you to import or export grade data;
- lets students see their grades, possibly in various ways;
- helps you identify students at risk; and
- makes it easier to coordinate and speed up grading with your TAs.

If you link the graded items to the grade book, when you enter the scores for student work into the LMS, it automatically adds the scores to the grade book. For example, if you link a discussion to a column in the grade book, and then give a student a grade for that discussion, it'll go into that column. This saves you time and effort, and eliminates the possibility that scores might be copied incorrectly. Scores can also be added to the grade book by multimedia objects or tests hosted by publishing companies.

Once you've entered students' scores, the grade book can do all your grading arithmetic, such as calculating average scores for different kinds of items, weighted and unweighted. Some can also do fancier calculations,

DOI: 10.4324/9781003161288-14

such as deriving students' letter grades based on ranges that you provide or ignoring students' lowest quiz scores.

The grade book also allows you to export the scores to do more sophisticated analysis and grading than your LMS supports. For example, you can use a spreadsheet to analyze the scores to determine if your TAs are grading comparably. You can import the results of your spreadsheet computations back into the grade book.

One of the biggest advantages of the grade book is that the LMS lets students see their scores (when you have authorized this). We recommend that you create calculated running average columns for each type of graded item, so your students will know how they're doing. For example, the grade book can calculate students' average quiz scores, as well as giving both you and your students running scores of how they're doing based on how much quizzes count in the course. Some grade book **add-ons** also show the distribution of their classmates' scores and where they stand. These can both be great motivators.

The grade book can also help you identify students who are at risk of failing or dropping the course. Running average scores for each type of **assessment** will show students who are not doing well on a specific type: For example, you may find students who are terrible at labs, but do well on exams. Similarly, you can look for students whose scores are declining significantly. You can use these to warn students who may not pass unless their grades improve.

The grade book is especially helpful when many TAs are grading assessments, because they can enter those grades directly. If there's a crunch at the end of the term, this'll help you get the grades in on time. Also, TAs are likely to know when students were in situations that impaired their performance. (For more on helping students, see Chapter 11.) The grade book can provide a place for them to record what has happened.

We have found that creating two columns is helpful. One is a text column for grade comments, and the other is a column for the TAs' suggested course grades. You should hide these columns from your students, and if you use the suggested grade column, we recommend that you also hide it from yourself until you have derived the final course grades. After that, compare your grades with those from your TAs. If any differ, try to figure out why. This simple method works well to ensure fair grading. (For more on working with your TAs, see Chapter 9.)

The grade book can also help you handle extra credit. One way is to add extra credit to a specific graded item, such an assignment or discussion. Another is to add extra credit to the final total score, which you can do by creating an extra-credit column and adding it to the weighted total score. One of the authors records all class contribution credits in a separate, extra-credit column, so he can take it into account when it's time to derive the final grades.

The grade book can also help you foster academic integrity by spotting students who do well on non-proctored items, such as assignments, but fail or do poorly under proctored conditions, such as exams.

14.2 How can I reward online students for insightful participation?

Productive student participation makes classes more interesting for students and you, and also serves to ensure academic integrity, as students who can answer questions have usually done their own work. You can encourage this by setting a good example and clear expectations, establishing grading **rubrics**, and giving prompt feedback (Poole, 2000).

Leading by example in your own teaching, asking questions and getting others involved in discussions (rather than droning on endlessly) is important in both **synchronous** and **asynchronous** sessions. When a student sparks discussion with a post or makes an insightful comment in a synchronous session that is well aligned with the learning objectives and helps their classmates learn, reply with praise and let everyone know right then that you'll be giving them class contribution credit for it.

Grading asynchronous contributions can take some care. If you grade your online discussions based just on the number of posts, you'll get many posts that do not contribute to learning, such as "I agree!" or "Great post!" If you grade based just on the length of the post, you'll receive submissions that are long, boring, and often off-topic. What you want to see are posts that demonstrate knowledge while contributing to everyone's learning. For example, a short, thoughtful post, raising a question that stimulates thoughtful replies, will earn full credit, while a long post with little pedagogic value may earn no credit.

You'll encourage useful discussion contributions by making sure your grading rubrics are clear and easily accessible (Kent et al., 2016). Discussion grading may be summarized in the syllabus, with details in the discussion grading rubric such as sample discussion posts, how you'd evaluate them, and the scores they'd receive. (For more on rubrics, see Appendix G.)

> Hint: We tell our students not to be afraid to ask "dumb questions" or give "dumb answers" that reveal gaps in their knowledge, because these help us learn what we need to address—we even give extra credit for them.

The more promptly you can provide your students with feedback and guidance, the more effective it will be in shaping their behavior.

14.3 How do I provide feedback when grading online student submissions?

When you or your TAs are grading, you should provide feedback any time you're deducting points (Eckstein, Bergin, & Sharp, 2002). Because this will usually be negative, you should try to balance this with positive comments for the parts of the submission that were well done. Sometimes the best feedback is a little guidance, with a request to resubmit a portion of the assignment.

Online tools allow you to communicate with your students in ways that you couldn't in an on-campus course. For example, you can incorporate audio and video comments when you're grading students' submissions. These let you walk quickly through a student's submission and explain in detail any strengths and any areas needing improvement. People speak several times faster than they type (Kalava et al., 2014; Miller et al., 1976), so you can give a lot more information in a short period of time. This more expressive feedback can also easily communicate nuances that are difficult to convey in text; tone of voice and facial expressions can say a lot. This helps your students feel more connected to you.

If you have doubts about students submitting their own work, a brief **videoconference** or telephone discussion lets you ask questions about their methodology, research methods, or how they arrived at their conclusions (2021). It can be useful to include a note in your syllabus that students may be contacted at any time and asked about their work.

14.4 How do I teach my online students about academic integrity?

To function well, a learning community must have a code of conduct that includes intellectual honesty (Guenin, 2005). Part of this code is to never represent someone else's ideas or work as your own. Academic integrity assures students that they'll be graded fairly, and that other students won't gain unfair advantage by cheating. The most common academic integrity problems arise when students plagiarize or otherwise cheat on assessments. Faculty have a responsibility for teaching academic integrity and enforcing it. (Techniques for assuring the academic integrity of tests and assignments are covered later in this chapter.)

We recommend that you include a summary of your academic integrity policy in your syllabus, and include links to your institution's complete academic integrity policies. The following example combines text from several of Boston University's Metropolitan College courses:

> This course is governed by the Academic Conduct Committee policies regarding plagiarism, which is defined as attempting to represent the work of another person as one's own. This includes copying, even with modifications, source code or data without crediting the source. You can discuss general ideas with other people, but the work you submit must be your own.

Many faculty emphasize the importance of academic integrity by requiring their students to read and acknowledge that they understand the applicable policies.

Hint: Consider requiring students to acknowledge or affirm that they have read and will follow your academic conduct code before they can access course content in your LMS.

You can model intellectual honesty for your students by citing sources in your lectures and slides. You should state clearly what you expect of your students and teach them when and how to cite their sources (Pino & Smith, 2003). You may also provide your students with a tutorial on citing sources and academic integrity using the conventions of your program. For example, if your program uses **APA style**, you may wish to refer your students to the tutorial at <apastyle.org>. One of the authors has developed a short self-assessment tutorial that teaches when and how to credit sources, and he requires that students earn at least 95 percent on its test before they submit any of their assignments.

We also recommend that you link to an **originality checker**, such as Turnitin or SafeAssign, in your course (for more on this, see later in this chapter). If you give your students an opportunity to see the results from an originality check of their work, they'll learn that good checkers catch plagiarism, including paraphrasing. This will encourage them to submit only their own work.

14.5 How do I review assignment solutions with students online and still ensure academic integrity?

In some disciplines, faculty may need to review assignment solutions with their students. However, this can compromise the academic integrity of the assignment if some students submit their solution after the review, or if your solution has been published on the web. A good technique for assuring the integrity of assignment solutions is to have an alternative for each of the assignments: You can require that students who haven't submitted by the time of the review do the alternative assignment.

> Hint: You don't need to create alternatives for all of your assignments in advance; you can just create them when needed, and also incorporate them into the course for future use.

One common way that students cheat on assignments is by obtaining solutions from websites that provide this as a service (Kitahara & Westfall, 2007). The solutions on cheating websites are often submitted by many students, so originality checkers will flag them. If there's any doubt, ask a student who's submitting after the review to explain their solution to you in a synchronous session.

> Hint: The current generation of cheating websites doesn't support video, and one of the authors has taken advantage of this by publishing the solutions to his assignments as videos embedded in the course.

14.6 How can I ensure that online students are doing their own assignments and projects?

Cheating on assignments and projects is rampant online. Students can submit their assignments or projects to websites that will match them with people who'll provide solutions for a fee (Morris, 2018). Competition has reduced the cost so much that students can afford to use these services often. There are three overall techniques that you can use to prevent this form of cheating and to detect it when it happens: Discussions with or presentations by your students; having milestone deliverables, such as drafts of papers; and using an originality checker.

If you discuss assignments and projects with your students, you'll know what they are thinking and working on, and they'll know that you know this, so they won't submit some else's work. You can go over assignments in synchronous sessions, asking each student how they're doing, and if there are any problems. This usually takes only a few minutes per student; if a student needs more time, it should be during office hours.

Students are most tempted to have someone else do their work when they get behind and feel desperate (Wilhoit, 1994). You can help keep them on track by requiring milestone deliverables and progress reports. These periodic check-ins can be done in the synchronous sessions described above, or more formally. If students' projects include a presentation, a good way to do the milestone check-ins is to have them present their progress to date (Born, 2003). These check-in presentations can consume a lot of faculty time, so you may wish to have them supervised by TAs (if you have them) and have them recorded for your review in case there are issues.

Once students have submitted their work, there are several ways to be sure that they're the ones who actually did it. You can start by running it through an originality checker to help identify plagiarism and paraphrasing—or you can have students submit it to the checker linked to your course. Originality checkers compare a paper's text to a database that includes previously submitted student papers, academic and commercial journals and publications, as well many websites, such as Wikipedia.

> Hint: If you're using an originality checker in such a way that your students' papers will be entered into its database, you should include a disclosure in your syllabus that you're doing this.

These tools can detect material that has been copied or paraphrased, but they can't detect an entirely original paper that has been written for the student by someone else. However, they still often detect papers written for payment, because people who write papers for students will often sell the same paper, sometimes with modifications, to many students.

Another approach to detecting material that has been copied is to paste a distinct phrase, including vocabulary or a type of punctuation that doesn't sound like your student (Heberling, 2002), from their submission into a search engine, such as Google. The less common the words and phrases are, the more specific the search results will be. This technique can be more effective at identifying plagiarism than originality checkers, because search engine crawlers index virtually the entire web.

There are additional ways that plagiarizing students can tip you off: One is inconsistent use of single and double quotes, as well as typefaces. If you see a paper using multiple styles, you should be suspicious that parts have been copied and pasted, because nobody makes this kind of mistake when typing a paper from scratch. Another is that sometimes students will copy and paste something from the web into Microsoft Word or another editor that retains hidden HTML, but presents it as ordinary text. The student won't realize it, but you can detect this by setting Word's preferences to display field codes or by pasting the content into a text editor.

Remember that preventing plagiarism is easier than dealing with it after it happens. If you provide your students access to the originality checker, they'll see that it identifies many sources, which often discourages them from even trying to submit plagiarized work.

14.7 How do I make it harder for my students to cheat on online tests?

Cheating on tests is common online and it's a major problem because it undermines the integrity of online education. Students can cheat on online tests in many ways (Olt, 2002), including:

- getting prior tests for the course;
- getting tests from a classmate who took them earlier;
- working on them with a classmate;
- having someone else take them; and
- looking up the answers.

The first two ways of cheating can be dealt with by giving students different tests. This is easier to do online than in the classroom, with a paper-based test, because LMSs let you create several questions that cover the same material, organized into question sets, with questions selected randomly for individual students. Table 14.1 illustrates five question sets, each containing three questions.

Table 14.1 Question sets

Question Set 1	Question Set 2	Question Set 3	Question Set 4	Question Set 5
Q 1.1	Q 2.1	Q 3.1	Q 4.1	Q 5.1
Q 1.2	Q 2.2	Q 3.2	Q 4.2	Q 5.2
Q 1.3	Q 2.3	Q 3.3	Q 4.3	Q 5.3

When students take a test based on these question sets, the LMS will randomly select questions, as illustrated in Table 14.2. It's likely that your students will receive different tests (Cizek, 1999; Cluskey et al., 2011).

Some faculty prefer to have 20 question sets, each composed of three questions. Different question sets can have different point values. For example, your test may include 10 **multiple-choice** questions worth five points each and one essay question worth 50 points. Students may still be able to cheat by getting prior tests, but they'll be much less useful, because most of the questions that they get on their test won't be on any given prior

Table 14.2 Student tests created from question sets

Student A	Student B	Student C	Student D	Student E
Q 1.1	Q 1.1	Q 1.3	Q 1.2	Q 1.3
Q 2.2	Q 2.1	Q 2.2	Q 2.3	Q 2.1
Q 3.2	Q 3.1	Q 3.2	Q 3.3	Q 3.3
Q 4.1	Q 4.3	Q 4.2	Q 4.1	Q 4.2
Q 5.3	Q 5.3	Q 5.2	Q 5.2	Q 5.3

test. If students work together on a test, they'll most likely get different questions, so they'll still have to work to answer most of them.

There are tradeoffs in the number of questions in a question set. The effort to create a test is mainly proportional to its number of questions. If there are too few questions in question sets, students will get tests that are more similar. We have found that having question sets containing three questions is a good compromise between cheating deterrence and ease of **development**. Question sets require more effort to create, but they can reduce your effort to update them between terms. If you use question sets, you can reuse tests without unduly compromising academic integrity.

You should try to create questions that are of comparable difficulty; you can check this by using the statistical analysis functions available in many LMSs. However, if there are a lot of questions in a question set and not many students in your course, some questions may not be answered by enough students to get good statistical results. You need about 20 responses to a question to get a usably accurate estimate of the mean score.

Online you can't prevent students from looking up the answers on the web unless you use a proctoring service or a **lockdown browser**. So, you should design questions that don't have simple, factual answers that can be retrieved by search, solving problems rather than recalling answers. For example, ask questions like "Which word is the subject of 'I love online education?'" or "Which of the following are reasons that Target did better than their competitors after COVID-19 hit?"

If you wish to use automatically graded questions, you can do this by posing problems, providing a list of possible answers or solutions, and asking students to choose the best one. It's easy to create unsearchable questions that are more difficult than searchable ones; the challenge is often creating unsearchable questions that are not too difficult for your students. Table 14.3 gives examples of creating unsearchable questions from searchable questions.

Table 14.3 Searchable questions and mechanisms for creating their unsearchable counterparts

Searchable questions	Unsearchable questions	Mechanism
Solve the equation x^2=-4	What number squared equals minus four?	words
What are the steps in backwards design?	In backwards design, what should be developed before assessments?	sequence
What is the international standard unit of mass?	The pound is to imperial measure as *what* in the metric system?	analogy
What is the French word for "small?"	In French, what is the opposite of "large?"	opposite

> Hint: Paste your questions into a search engine and see if what is returned will help students answer them.

One of the challenges of online tests is that we don't see our students taking them, so we can't be sure that the students who are getting grades for tests are the ones who took them, or that they were working alone. One solution is to have tests proctored, with positive student identification. (For more on proctoring tests, see later in this chapter.) Another solution is to include a statement in your syllabus that if there is any doubt about a student having done their own work, they'll be given an oral exam on the topic (Cole & Kiss, 2000).

14.8 How can exams be proctored online, and what are the tradeoffs?

You can randomize your tests and make students use lockdown browsers, but unless they're being proctored, students can always sit next to each other and help each other answer the questions. When exams are administered on campus, either faculty or a proctor is in the room observing the students, to ensure that they adhere to the exam rules. Exams can also be proctored online.

Proctoring online consists of ensuring that:

- the person taking the exam is actually the student who's getting credit;
- students only use materials that are allowed for the exam; and
- students taking the exam aren't receiving help from anyone else.

Students can be identified by having them present approved photo IDs, or by biometric techniques such as fingerprints, or by facial or speaker recognition. Some of these techniques require baseline data, such as a photograph or fingerprint that is known to be of the student. For example, use of a photograph requires:

- baseline photo provided with the application for admission to the program;
- photo taken on campus; and
- driver's license or passport shown during exam.

The cost and quality of online proctoring services vary widely. There are limits to the number of students that can be proctored by each person, so the cost of human proctoring makes it more expensive than automated proctoring. We have found that human proctoring is roughly three times as expensive as automated proctoring.

Less expensive online proctoring services depend on automation. The main automation technologies are lockdown browsers that prevent students from accessing anything other than their exam, video and audio recording of the students and their screens during the exam, and gaze surveillance software to flag times when students look away from their screens. Unfortunately, the most that automated software can do is identify segments of exam recordings that need to be reviewed by a human proctor, and there may be many such segments for each student. Automation reduces the up-front costs, but must be balanced against the cost of staff and faculty time needed to review these flagged items.

There are academic integrity tradeoffs in using expensive, higher-quality versus inexpensive, lower-quality online proctoring. High-quality online proctoring is sufficiently expensive that most institutions only use it for comprehensive final exams or exams for certification, leaving quizzes and midterms un-proctored. Faculty generally weight proctored assessments more heavily than un-proctored; they and their administrators need to determine which assessments should be proctored, and how.

If the cost of commercial proctoring is a problem, your institution can use one of the less-expensive automated proctoring services, or you and your TAs can do it (if you have any). You can treat an exam like a synchronous session, where all of the students log into a videoconferencing system while they take the exam, and faculty watch and record students. The main disadvantages to this approach are:

- You don't get complete recordings of students' computer screens and audio.

- Students can take the exam only when faculty are available to proctor.
- If there are many students it takes a lot of faculty time.

It's critical that any online proctoring include a recording of the exam session that can be used in a hearing or court of law. There have been well-publicized incidents where institutions have accused students of cheating based on automated proctoring, when the events that triggered the accusations turned out to have been generated internally, within the LMS, or the evidence recorded by the automatic proctoring system was found to be inadequate to justify a student-conduct hearing (Hussein et al., 2020; Singer & Krolik, 2021).

Proctoring online exams takes more planning than proctoring on campus. Commercial proctoring services must be notified weeks in advance regarding the length of the exam, the number of students, and the exam rules. Most vendors require that students have a webcam and microphone. Proctoring services generally require that all students in a course take an exam with the same rules, though they should be able to support some students being allowed more time as a disability accommodation.

Proctored online exams have two kinds of policies or rules—policies common to all exams and rules specific to an exam. The following policies for students are used by Boston University's Office of Distance Education:

- Your computer must be connected to a power source.
- Only one monitor is allowed. If you have more than one monitor, you'll need to unplug the extras and move them away from your workspace.
- Your desk and work area must be cleared. This includes any written material, regardless if it's for class or not. If the exam allows printed materials, you must show them to the proctor.
- You'll have supplied your phone number during exam registration. If the proctor isn't able to reach you through the proctoring software, they'll call your phone, so it should be in the same room, but not on your desk.
- You must be alone in the room. If someone might enter the room, such as a child or spouse, please let your proctor know this beforehand. The proctor will probably ask you to scan the room with your webcam to make sure the person is no longer there.
- You're not allowed to talk, except to the proctor.
- You're not allowed to leave your seat. If you have to use the restroom or adjust anything in the room, you must let the proctor know. The proctor will make a note of it and may ask you to scan the room with your webcam.

- Webcam, speakers, and microphone must remain on throughout the test, so the proctor can see you and contact you if necessary.
- The proctor must be able to see you for the duration of the test. The proctor may ask you to adjust your webcam.

In addition to these common online proctoring rules, you'll need to provide the proctor with rules specific to your exam. The following checklist is an example of what proctoring services need to know about an exam:

- Exam starts <date> at <time>
- Exam ends <date> at <time>
- Exam duration: <#> minutes
- Use of the physical and/or ebook textbook is allowed: <Y/N>
- Use of a standard handheld and/or desktop calculator is allowed: <Y/N>
- Online calculators are not permitted: <Y/N>
- Use of any printed and/or electronic materials (such as PDFs) is allowed. This includes the following: <List of allowed materials>
- Use of the following software is allowed: <List of allowed software>
- Use of three pieces of blank scratch paper is allowed: <Y/N>

14.9 How do I encourage online students to turn on their webcams?

Faculty can encourage students to turn on their webcams by setting a good example—using one themselves—and by awarding class contribution credit for students who use them.

Many students are uncomfortable when they first use a webcam in a class. They may feel self-conscious, knowing that their classmates and faculty are seeing them. Some students may not want to turn on their webcams because they don't want to be watched; they may simply dislike it, or dislike feeling obligated to look attentive for the camera. Other students aren't confident that they'll look good on a webcam, and they're uncomfortable with not knowing when people are looking at them. When students overcome this anxiety, they learn that their classmates are in similar situations and they quickly become comfortable with it. The challenge for faculty is just getting them over the hump to try it. Since the pandemic, of course, many more students have experience with using their webcams, making this task easier.

You can help them overcome this anxiety by creating a videoconference practice room to experiment with their cameras. You also can help them by offering to come to your synchronous sessions 15 minutes early to assist them with their audio and cameras. If a student has difficulty with their camera, and you can't help them, refer them to tech support.

When students and faculty use their webcams, it helps everyone understand each other, feel more comfortable communicating, and it helps build community. Webcams help faculty show care for their students by smiles and other body language. They also help faculty know how their students are doing, because they can see when their students smile, nod, or look puzzled or uncertain. Webcams also help students establish relationships with each other, which fosters a stronger learning community.

There are situations for students to not use their webcams, and you should be sensitive to this. It might be because they're listening while doing something like making dinner, and they don't want people to know what they are doing.

Sometimes a student can't allow their face to be broadcast for security reasons: They may work for a government agency, need to avoid a stalker or harassing ex, or be in witness protection. If a student tells you about this, let them use a stock photography image of someone else in place of their webcam feed, so it won't look as strange to their classmates as a blank box.

References

Born, A. D. (2003). Teaching tip: How to reduce plagiarism. *Journal of Information Systems Education, 14*(3), 223–224.

Cizek, G. J. (1999). *Cheating on tests: How to do it, detect it, and prevent it.* Mahwah, NJ: Lawrence Erlbaum.

Cluskey, G. R., Jr., Ehlen, C. R., & Raiborn, M. H. (2011). Thwarting online exam cheating without proctor supervision. *Journal of Academic and Business Ethics, 4*(1), 1–7.

Cole, S., & Kiss, E. (2000). What can we do about student cheating? *About Campus, 5*(2), 5–12.

Eckstein, J., Bergin, J., & Sharp, H. (2002). *Feedback Patterns*. Proceedings from European Conference on Pattern Languages of Programs.

Guenin, L. M. (2005). Intellectual honesty. *Synthese, 145*, 177–232.

Heberling, M. (2002). Maintaining academic integrity in online education. *Online Journal of Distance Learning Administration, V*(1), 1–6.

Hussein, M. J., Yusuf, J., Deb, A. S., Fong, L., & Naidu, S. (2020). An evaluation of online proctoring tools. *Open Praxis, 12*(4), 509–525.

Kalava, A., Ravindranath, S., Bronshteyn, I., Munjal, R. S., SchianodiCola, J., & Yarmush, J. M. (2014). Typing skills of physicians in training. *Journal of Graduate Medical Education, 6*(1), 155–157.

Kent, C., Laslo, E., & Rafaeli, S. (2016). Interactivity in online discussions and learning outcomes. *Computers & Education, 97*, 116–128.

Kitahara, R. T., & Westfall, F. (2007). Promoting academic integrity in online distance learning courses. *MERLOT Journal of Online Learning and Teaching, 3*(3), 265–276.

Miller, N., Maruyama, G., Beaber, R. J., & Valone, K. (1976). Speed of speech and persuasion. *Journal of personality and social psychology, 34*(4), 615–624.

Morris, E. J. (2018). Academic integrity matters: five considerations for addressing contract cheating. *International Journal for Educational Integrity, 14*, 1–12.

Olt, M. R. (2002). Ethics and distance education: Strategies for minimizing academic dishonesty in online assessment. *Online Journal of Distance Learning Administration, 5*(3), 1–7.

Pino, N. W., & Smith, W. L. (2003). College students and academic dishonesty. *College Student Journal, 37*(4), 490–500.

Poole, D. M. (2000). Student participation in a discussion-oriented online course: A case study. *Journal of Research on Computing in Education, 33*(2), 162–177.

Singer, N., & Krolik, A. (2021). Online Cheating Charges Upend Dartmouth Medical School. *The New York Times*. Retrieved from www.nytimes.com/2021/05/09/technology/dartmouth-geisel-medical-cheating.html.

Wilhoit, S. (1994). Helping students avoid plagiarism. *College teaching, 42*(4), 161–164.

Chapter 15

Making online courses better

In this chapter we answer questions about how to evaluate online courses and identify ways to make them better. We describe ways to determine how well courses meet students' needs and contribute to their programs.

15.1 How can I teach my online course better next time?

Student evaluations are critical for improving courses, and you should get them shortly after you teach a course. Some are easy to interpret. For example, if many students complain that you take too long to reply to emails, it's obvious how you can improve. Similarly, if students complain that it takes too long to complete an assignment, you can split or change it to make better use of their time.

Some evaluations are harder to interpret and learn from. For example, some students may write rave reviews about a **learning activity**, while other students find it a waste of time. If it isn't obvious how to respond, talk with an **instructional designer** or faculty with online experience. Sometimes, if a student comment is inconsistent with other feedback, the best practice is to just see if it comes up again. If so, address it later.

Another way to obtain guidance for improving your course is informal peer review. This can be as simple as asking a colleague how to improve some aspect of your course. A more structured approach is to sit down with a colleague and review an archived course and its student evaluations, discussing the issues. If you're new to teaching online, it's good to confer with more experienced faculty, either at your own institution or elsewhere. You can also get help from professional organizations, such as MERLOT <merlot.org>, the Online Learning Consortium <onlinelearningconsortium.org>, and the United States Distance Learning Association <usdla.org>. Don't overlook the advantages of talking with other faculty who are also new to online.

DOI: 10.4324/9781003161288-15

They may not have more experience than you do, but they may know how to address your issues.

Formal peer reviews occur when a program is up for accreditation, or, more commonly, when student evaluations or complaints identify significant problems. One of the authors was the director of a program in which faculty used an undergraduate-level textbook for a graduate course, and students howled. This led to a formal review of the course, which concluded that the content was not at the appropriate level, so the entire course needed to be redeveloped.

After you've gotten these evaluations and reviews, you might want to address issues they raised by teaching some material in a different way. If you pilot a new method in just one area of your course, this will allow you to get experience with it and learn how well it works before making the changes everywhere. This will help minimize your risk and effort.

For example, one of your colleagues may say that **formative evaluations** help students learn difficult concepts, and you can add them to an area in your course where your students have struggled. You can design them so that students can choose whether or not to take them; students will skip them if they're not helpful. If they do help, consider adding them throughout the course.

15.2 How can I use student feedback and evaluations to improve my online course?

The effectiveness of teaching is measured by how it helps students learn, so guidance from students should play a central role in shaping your course (McKone, 1999). Your students can help you improve your course by providing suggestions or feedback (Brew, 2008). You'll get some of this information while your course is running, and some afterwards, in student evaluations and peer review.

As a course is running, you'll get student feedback as to what is working and what isn't. On campus, you can usually figure out what works and what doesn't right away simply by observing your students; online, without subtle cues like body language, such observation is more difficult, but there are more opportunities to learn what works and what doesn't. You can:

- Ask your students questions about the subject matter in **synchronous** sessions. This will tell you how well they are learning the material, and help you identify any misunderstandings.
- Ask your students how well the course is working for them. If they trust you, they'll provide good, nuanced guidance, as well as whether or not

they're enjoying it. This is important, because students learn best when they are enjoying their studies (Ferris & Gerber, 1996).
- Provide "Suggestions for course improvement" discussion forums. These can elicit good feedback, particularly if they are anonymous.
- Ask students' opinions in surveys about a particular element while the course is running (Lewis, 2001). Your questions should be designed to be answered quickly, so they don't take much of your students' time, and they should focus on things that you need to know about the course, such as how the experimental course element is working. One advantage of surveys is that they can seed dialogues between you and your students.

Your students will also help you indirectly, by how they choose to spend their time in the course and how well they learn the material:

- Your formative evaluation logs, if they exist, will tell you which questions many students get wrong.
- Your **LMS** and server usage statistics may tell you how much time your students spent on each activity. Your students will have spent more time on activities that they enjoyed or found useful.
- Your quiz and exam results will tell you how much they've learned and where you may need to cover material again, or differently.

> Hint: Don't be afraid to try new ways of teaching. If some **asynchronous** content doesn't work out, you can always cover it synchronously.

Once a course has run, you'll receive feedback in the student evaluations. Sometimes students are reluctant to provide honest feedback before they've received their final grades for the course, because they're afraid that it will affect their grades. However, many institutions require that student evaluations be completed before the final exam, because if students complete their evaluations right after it, they'll mainly be responding to their final exam experience. If you want feedback on the final exam, you may need to solicit it by email or survey.

Your student evaluations should include questions about different aspects of the course, such as what they liked or didn't about the lectures, discussions, quizzes, and assignments, and how they could be improved. They should also include a comment section where students can provide any feedback they wish.

Students take courses for many different reasons, and they have different backgrounds, so their feedback can be surprisingly varied (Nasser & Fresko, 2002). When faculty see their first student evaluations, they're often surprised and don't know how to respond when different students love and hate the same aspect of the course. You need to interpret your student evaluations using something like a statistical measure. If almost all of the students love some aspect of the course, but one or two students hate it, don't be discouraged; just go with the majority.

Rarely, it happens that about equal numbers of students love and hate the same thing. If it does, consider creating options for different students. For example, if a third of your students love a new assignment and a third hate it, you can create two assignments that cover the same material, and let your students choose between them. It's generally best to have multiple explanations for key subject matter, anyway. If some of your students don't like how you presented something and complain about it, you can usually correct this by adding explanations or examples. If you have widely divergent feedback on something, and can't figure out how to address it, you should ask an instructional designer or more experienced faculty, if possible.

If your institution collects data from graduates ("**outcome analysis**") and shares it with faculty, you may obtain helpful information. Outcome analysis answers questions about whether the **curriculum** as a whole meets the students' expectations and actual needs, so much of the information may not apply specifically to your course. The outcomes may identify topics that should be added to the curriculum because students need them, and topics that no longer need to be covered because they don't. You should try to analyze this data with your colleagues to determine what should be addressed and in which courses. (For more on outcome analysis, see Hillman, Schudy, & Temkin, 2021.)

15.3 How do I determine if my online course meets its learning objectives?

You need to measure how well your students are meeting your learning objectives. You may think that your course has met an objective because you covered that topic in a lecture, but then you learn that your students haven't mastered it. This could be because your course had no discussions or assignments covering it, because the asynchronous lecture material lacked formative evaluations, or because you didn't cover this material in a synchronous session to be sure that your students got it. In some cases, a course can meet its objectives for one group of students, but not for another. You can address this by adding learning activities for the students who need them.

You can identify areas where your students meet the learning objectives, and those where they don't, by ensuring that your course:

- has formative evaluations that cover the key objectives;
- includes assignments covering the objectives;
- has quizzes and other graded **assessments** that test objectives; and
- has a final exam that covers key objectives.

Some of the assessments should come early enough to give students and you feedback in time to help them, for example, in a synchronous session. This practice, of monitoring your students' learning related to the objectives, should continue throughout the course. It's also a good practice to review your final exam results and identify any questions where your students didn't do as well as you expected. Examine the learning objectives that each of these questions assesses and strengthen the areas where students haven't mastered the material.

15.4 How do I know if my online course needs to be updated?

Often the issue is not whether or not your course needs updating, but if you have time to update it. Many updates require significant effort, and you'll need to decide which of the changes to include as part of an update and which to defer. This will also help you determine how much of your time updates will take and which ones you can complete.

The following questions will help you decide if your course needs to be updated:

- Are there errors in the course material?
- Is there a better book for my course?
- Do my students need to learn something different?
- Would a different sequencing of the material work better?
- Would different teaching methods improve my course?
- Have students suggested changes to the course material?
- Can my use of technology be improved to help students learn?
- Do curriculum changes require modifications to my course?

While the answer to any one of these questions may lead you to decide to update your course, more commonly a combination of factors will shape your decision. Whether and what to update depends on the cost and the benefits of the updates.

The effort required to update your course will also depend on its design. If each topic is covered in a single **module**, updates will only affect them. However, if topics thread through the modules of your course, changes may cascade or be required in many places.

> Hint: One approach is to list updates in priority order, with estimates of the level of effort, taking into account tasks which must be completed together. Then, when you're implementing those changes, start from the top of the list and work your way down. When you run out of time, stop and leave the remaining items for your next update.

If there are easily corrected errors in your course material, such as typos in text, illustrations, or video captions, you should correct them right away, if possible. In some programs, you can do this yourself, but in others, you'll need to ask an instructional designer or media specialist to add it to their work queue.

Changes to textbooks can require either minor or major updates. For example, if a new edition of the old textbook has come out and the old one is no longer available, you'll need to update your course, but the effort to do this is usually modest and the benefit great. If you need to change to an entirely different textbook, that may require much more effort, moving material in lectures so it aligns well with the chapter sequence of the new book, changing references to the book, and changing some content. This can require fully half as much effort as the original course **development**.

Often faculty discover that they need to cover something that is not currently in the course, or that something in the course is no longer useful to the students. Student needs may change, or the discipline may evolve. These updates can usually be made incrementally, but sometimes they require major rewrites. For example, one of the authors worked with his colleagues to update their database courses when big data databases became mainstream, and students needed to learn about them.

Sometimes faculty think that covering topics or learning activities in a different order will work better. Resequencing some of the elements in your course will probably require rewriting some of the course content, such as transition material. If the elements that are being resequenced are in the same module, the effort is usually modest. If they're in different modules, you'll also need to update the assignments and assessments.

At times faculty may want to try an online teaching technology that they've learned about, and this may require course updates. While basic teaching methods are fairly stable, technologies to implement them online constantly improve, so faculty may wish to update their courses to take advantage. For example, one of the authors originally developed videos for his probability and statistics course using a chalkboard; five years later he redid them using a whiteboard, making the problems easier to read. He is now redoing them again, using a lightboard, which makes the problems even easier to read, while letting his students see his face while he writes, rather than the back of his head. Updating these videos won't require his students to update their computers, but they'll make his course better.

> Hint: Be careful not to be seduced by flashy new technologies that require your students to have fast computers and internet connections or special peripherals.

Student suggestions for course updates or improvements are valuable, but students may not understand how the changes would affect other students, the course as a whole, and the curriculum. They may also fail to reckon with the amount of time and effort changes can take to implement. Faculty need to decide if the suggestions will help enough students, if a given change will disrupt the coherence and flow of the course, and if the improvement is worth the effort.

Sometimes changes to a curriculum may add material to a course, delete it, or move substantial content between courses, requiring major updates. If the changes that you need to make are significant, you need to think carefully about how long it will take and create an update plan and schedule. (For more on course development plans and schedules, see Chapter 5.)

15.5 How can I work with other faculty to improve my online courses?

When other faculty review the courses that you have developed, they'll inevitably see things that you didn't and be able to improve them. When you're reviewing a course developed by other faculty, you'll also see things that they didn't. When you have several faculty who are qualified to teach and update a course, they should take turns updating it, when possible. If they work well together, over time the course will have the best that each of them can produce.

There are three main ways in which faculty can help each other make courses better: Improving the writing, the content, and the curriculum. Many people find that having someone else critique their writing can be embarrassing or even frightening. Remember that it's better to have someone friendly find errors before your students do. Be grateful, not defensive or offended.

If you have taught a course recently and have student evaluations, meet with one or two experienced faculty to go over them together and see how you can improve the content. They may have a different perspective that will help you identify the most productive changes to the course and how you teach it. (For more on interpreting student evaluations, see earlier in this chapter.)

Faculty who have curriculum responsibilities can also help you improve the integration of the course into the curriculum. Some improvements to a course may involve making changes to other courses or programs, such as moving material from one course to another, adding or deleting material, combining courses, and adding or deleting courses. Because changes beyond the scope of a course often require substantial curriculum updates, they can be done as part of a periodic curriculum review process, which involves many faculty.

15.6 How can I make my online course fit better into the program?

Like on-campus courses, an online course is usually part of a program curriculum, and it should be designed to support and be supported by other courses in that program. There are many aspects to fitting a course into a program. Some of them involve the design of the curriculum as a whole, while others involve the design and implementation of the specific course.

When a curriculum is designed, faculty allocate primary responsibility for most learning objectives to individual courses. For example, an undergraduate curriculum may allocate responsibility for English writing proficiency to a first-year English course.

Learning objectives of a curriculum may also be allocated to more than one course. For example, a college curriculum may allocate key mathematical literacy learning objectives to each of several introductory math courses and require that students take at least one of them. Sometimes learning objectives are sequenced at the curriculum level and course sequences and prerequisites are derived from this.

The key learning objectives for your course should be in your syllabus, and should be covered in both synchronous and asynchronous lectures. When you're developing and teaching a course, you should consider the following:

- If your course has prerequisite courses, examine them to avoid unnecessary duplication of content.
- Make sure that your students master the program learning objectives allocated to your course.

- If your course is a prerequisite for other courses, make sure that your students have mastered the topics that they'll need for later courses.

When you're developing your course, your syllabus should include a short section on the roles of the course in the program and curriculum, and you should also summarize it in your introductory lecture.

When students study the material in your course, they'll need to integrate it in their minds with the material they have already studied and be able to integrate future material with what you teach them. You can help them with this mental integration by including a little of the content of students' prior courses in your course. You can also help your students bridge the gap between courses by reminding them of what they have studied and by telling them when they'll learn more about some topics in an upcoming course. You should have just enough duplication to help your students put the concepts together.

> Hint: Sometimes there is a need to cover some material that is also taught in other courses; this most commonly occurs with introductory material. You can easily insert a noncredit "**Module 0: Prerequisite Review**" for students who want or need to go over prerequisite material. (For more on this, see Appendix B.)

References

Brew, L. S. (2008). The role of student feedback in evaluating and revising a blended learning course. *The Internet and Higher Education, 11*(2), 98–105.

Ferris, J., & Gerber, R. (1996). Mature-age students' feelings of enjoying learning in a further education context. *European Journal of Psychology of Education, 11*(1), 79–96.

Hillman, D., Schudy, R., & Temkin, A. (2021). *Best Practices for Administering Online Programs*. New York: Routledge.

Lewis, K. G. (2001). Using midsemester student feedback and responding to it. *New Directions for Teaching and Learning, 87*, 33–44.

McKone, K. E. (1999). Analysis of student feedback improves instructor effectiveness. *Journal of Management Education, 23*(4), 396–415.

Nasser, F., & Fresko, B. (2002). Faculty views of student evaluation of college teaching. *Assessment & Evaluation in Higher Education, 27*(2), 187–198.

Appendices

Certain topics recur in many answers, so we put them here to avoid unnecessary duplication.

Appendix A

Creating asynchronous lectures

This appendix covers the process of creating **asynchronous** lectures and what goes into them. The roles of asynchronous lectures in your courses and related considerations are covered in the main text.

Asynchronous lectures should be like engaging websites, where the content is the course material (McCabe & Hobohm, 2012). Just as there are many kinds of websites, there can be many kinds of asynchronous content, but most are primarily text with **embedded objects**, such as images and videos. The basic structure of a typical asynchronous course and its elements are illustrated in Figure A.1.

Unfortunately, creating asynchronous lectures requires more effort than preparing for **synchronous** lectures. Faculty who are used to lecturing on campus speak about 7,500 words per hour (Miller et al., 1976), so if you speak for 30 hours in a course, you'll have said around 225,000 words. Writing is more compact than speech; our typical courses have between 25,000–50,000 words, while our courses with the most content have about 100,000 words. Essentially, writing a lecture is like writing a chapter for a textbook. Students expect written lectures to be of textbook quality, so you should write carefully and have someone review your work.

There are a number of practical steps that you should take before you begin writing your lecture (these are described in detail in Chapter 5):

- Decide what your students need to know and need to be able to do. These should be expressed as learning objectives and measured by **assessments**.
- Create **module maps** listing the learning objectives and what you know about the topics.
    o Fill them in with **learning activities**, assessments, and assignments.
    o Identify significant graphics, video, and other learning objects that you'll want to include; this is particularly important if you'll need to have other people develop them.

Appendices 157

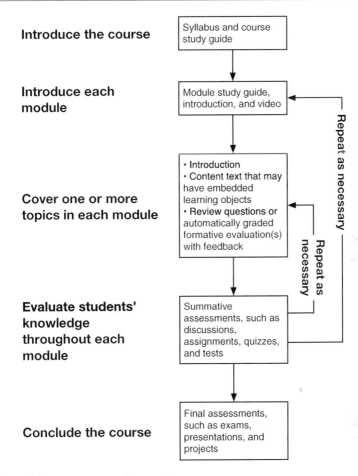

Figure A.1 Basic structure of an asynchronous course.

- Compile your module maps into a **course map**. It's useful to compare module maps for consistency across your course.
- Use the module and course maps to outline your asynchronous lectures and provide pedagogic context. These will help ensure that you cover the material that your students need to succeed in the assessments. It'll also help you see the big picture of your lecture, stay on track, and avoid digressions.
- Identify the course template, if available, that you'll use to ensure that your lecture is consistent with others in the course and program.

Once you know what you need to cover and have your course map set up as a basic outline, you can begin writing.

There are several ways to write the text portions of the lecture content of your asynchronous course. This text may ultimately become paragraphs, diagrams, or video scripts, but the words still have to be written. There are several techniques for creating the text:

- Most faculty just write their lectures based on the course map, or, if they've taught the course before, from their slides (see more on this, below).
- If you already teach your course on campus or synchronously, you can record your lectures and have them transcribed to create a first draft.
- If your course is new or you don't have an opportunity to record yourself lecturing, pretend that you're lecturing and record that.
- Combine these approaches: Check your course map and record your lectures, then read your slides and listen to the recording (or read the transcript of it) to prepare yourself for writing the text.

You can't just dump a transcript of your recorded lecture into your course and expect good results. Only exceptional faculty lecture in anything close to book-quality text. Don't be surprised when transcriptions of your lectures look shockingly bad compared to the polished writing in a textbook. This is normal; virtually everyone's speech looks terrible when it's transcribed. Give yourself plenty of time to edit the transcripts and clean up your false starts, digressions, and half-finished thoughts, plus time to polish the good parts.

Similarly, working from slides, like PowerPoint, is tricky. They can be very helpful when you are lecturing on campus or synchronously online, but they shouldn't normally be a part of your asynchronous lectures. While you can often incorporate graphics and images from them, we discourage you from using slides as a drop-in replacement for written asynchronous lectures.

During the pandemic, when many faculty were forced to go online with almost no preparation time, some recorded audio over their slides and used them as asynchronous lectures. This is entirely understandable as a desperation move, but in general it isn't a great solution: Although it contains some elements of a live lecture, it doesn't have any real interactivity, while it does have all the drawbacks of making students watch a long video.

An asynchronous lecture that is primarily slides won't contain many of the lecturing activities you do on campus without even thinking about them, such as:

- introducing the slides to give them context;
- explaining the relationships between the slides, expanding their bullet points to full explanations;

- asking your students questions to see if they understand;
- soliciting student comments;
- answering questions;
- humanizing asides;
- writing on the board; or
- briefly changing topics to keep your students' attention.

When you're using slides, one of the main differences between teaching on campus and writing an asynchronous lecture is that you'll need to write out or illustrate all of these elements in your text.

As you write and edit, keep in mind what else should be in your asynchronous lecture:

- introduction that defines its scope;
- introductory video;
- sections covering the topics—the text of the actual subject matter, plus **learning objects**, such as:
    - instructional illustrations and/or animations;
    - graphic elements taken from PowerPoint and similar slides;
    - short videos; and
- **Formative evaluations.**

Most elements in your online lecture should be introduced so that students understand why they're there, how they'll help them learn, and how to use them.

Your personal, introductory video is where you can really convey your passion for the subject at hand. Tell a cool story, like the time you solved a tricky problem. If you have good pictures to add, all the better.

Next comes the meat and potatoes of the course, your deathless prose, ornamented with learning objects such as illustrations, animations, and graphics taken from slides.

You might also think about augmenting your text with short videos of yourself lecturing ("short" meaning five minutes or less), to give students a chance to learn the content in a different mode. They can read the content in text or watch and listen to you. If you don't have time to record these the first time your course runs, it's easy to add them later. (For more on videos, see Chapter 6.)

Finally, formative evaluations provide a way for students to see what they have mastered and what they need to study. We include them at the bottom of each page of our courses after concepts are introduced. They are usually just a few automatically graded questions with feedback. (For more on formative evaluations, see Appendix E.)

Conversely, you also need to remember what shouldn't be in your asynchronous lecture, and be on the lookout for:

- long videos;
- images containing only text;
- due dates;
- grade weights;
- **rubrics;** and
- **summative assessments.**

Avoid long videos—unless you're teaching a course on movies—because students will stop watching them after a few minutes, unless you add questions to them to help engage students (Geri, Winer, & Zaks, 2017). And by "few" we mean ten minutes, tops, and preferably five minutes or less.

Make sure you don't have any images containing only text, because they aren't searchable or accessible. The text belongs in your lecture.

Rather than sprinkling due dates throughout your lecture, put them only in the module **study guides**. This will ensure that when your course runs again you only need to change them in one place, and you won't have conflicting information in the course for your students to ask you about. (For more on study guides, see Chapter 6.)

Similarly, grade weights should only be in the syllabus, so if they change when the course runs again, you'll only need to change them in one place. If you have to change them in lots of places, you'll inevitably miss one and students will get confused and ask you about it.

Students care about the grading rubrics when they're doing graded activities, but they don't care about them so much when they're just reading the lectures. Therefore, rubrics should be linked to the course or included in the assignment instructions, but should not be embedded in the lecture. This also allows rubrics to be changed independently, without modifying the lecture. (For more on rubrics, see Appendix G.)

Summative assessments, such as assignments and instructions on how to do them, should not be embedded in your lectures. Assignments should be self-contained, including their instructions, and linked to the course. Similarly, quizzes and tests go in the **LMS**, and should be linked to the course.

If you can't get all the asynchronous lecture content written before the course launches, you can write the later lectures while the course is running and post them for your students. This is difficult because you'll need to write whole lectures while you're busy teaching.

When you've finished writing and editing your asynchronous lectures, you should check one more time to make sure that they cover everything that your students need to know to do well on the assessments, and that the assessments cover everything you want your students to learn.

If you have access to an **instructional designer** or TA, they may help you put your lectures into the LMS, but faculty usually need to do this by themselves.

References

Geri, N., Winer, A., & Zaks, B. (2017). Challenging the six-minute myth of online video lectures: Can interactivity expand the attention span of learners. *Online Journal of Applied Knowledge Management, 5*(1), 101–111.

McCabe, B. K., & Hobohm, C. (2012). *Promoting asynchronous interactivity of recorded lectures in blended learning environments.* Proceedings from Annual Conference of the Australasian Society for Computers in Learning in Tertiary Education: Future Challenges, Sustainable Futures.

Miller, N., Maruyama, G., Beaber, R. J., & Valone, K. (1976). Speed of speech and persuasion. *Journal of personality and social psychology, 34*(4), 615–624.

Appendix B

Integrating prerequisite review material—Module 0

This appendix covers techniques you can use to include prerequisite review material in your **asynchronous** lectures.

By incorporating review material in your courses during **development**, you'll be ready to support students who aren't adequately prepared. We've discovered that a good design includes a "**Module 0: Prerequisite Review**" as the first **module** of many courses. If you include it in your asynchronous lectures, you won't have to spend nearly as much time reviewing material your students should already have known in **synchronous** lectures or office hours.

> Hint: Faculty who've taught the course before will often know where their students need additional preparation.

Module 0 should contain a comprehensive self-**assessment**, with feedback, so that students can quickly check if they're prepared to take the course or not. You can use the same self-assessment at the end of the module, so that students can verify that they've learned the material and are now ready.

When you're creating the prerequisite review material, what you do is largely determined by what's available in the prerequisite courses. Unless the prerequisite course is badly mis-aligned with your course (or is just a weak course, for whatever reason), you may be able to take the most important material from those courses into Module 0.

For example, if the prerequisite course has a lecture, or a part of a lecture, that will help prepare your students, the best approach may be to copy it into Module 0. You should be selective in what you take, including only the material that students need for your course; our experience has been that only a fraction of prerequisite content is essential in more advanced courses. If the prerequisite course already has automatically graded assessments with feedback, such as **LMS** quizzes, you may also be able to copy these over to Module 0, perhaps deleting questions that your students don't need.

> Hint: The customary academic protocol is for faculty to request permission to copy material from another faculty's course, and for that faculty to approve graciously. Faculty love being cited, so they rarely say no.

However, if the prerequisite course material is unusable for any reason, you'll just have to write the review material from scratch.

Underprepared students often have little time to catch up, so you should design Module 0 to make best use of their time. Self-assessments, with feedback that serves as teaching material, are very efficient. If students get something wrong, it gives them what they need to know. If they get a question right, they'll move on to the next question, without needing to read the feedback.

> Hint: If possible, provide students access to the prerequisite review before the course opens. The easiest option is to allow students into the course before it officially opens. If your institution's policies don't allow this, you may be able to make the review material available as a single-module course in the LMS.

You can also embed remedial material throughout your asynchronous lectures. For example, you can include help links or buttons that bring up definitions and remedial content. (For more on helping struggling students, see Chapter 11.)

Appendix C

Conducting synchronous sessions

Synchronous sessions can serve many different pedagogic roles; how you conduct them depends on what you're trying to accomplish. Table C.1 lists common types of synchronous sessions and how you run them.

Course introduction: The course introduction summarizes the course learning objectives, policies, and expectations. It should be done on the first day of the course and you shouldn't usually spend more than 30 minutes on it, unless students have questions. It should cover:

- relationships between this course and others in the **curriculum**;
- grading standards and **rubrics**;
- an explicit discussion of plagiarism and how to avoid it; and
- the number of hours that most students will need to study.

Module introduction: The module introduction is designed to prepare your students for the module and to get them excited about the material in it. Your students will respond better and learn more if your module introduction communicates your passion about the material. It should be done on the first day devoted to the module, and you should spend 10–50 minutes on it. It should cover:

- relationships between this module and others;
- key points of the module; and
- assignments and **assessments**.

Lectures: Synchronous lectures give your students opportunities to ask you questions and let you know what they need you to cover more. While students can always ask questions **asynchronously**, sometimes they can be unclear themselves on what they're asking, and it often takes some back-and-forth to figure out what they actually need. This sort of negotiation of meaning can be done much more efficiently in synchronous sessions. Faculty

Table C.1 Common types of synchronous sessions and how to run them

Type of session	How to run them	When	Length
course introduction	welcome students and summarize learning objectives, policies, and expectations	first day of the course	15–30 minutes
module introductions	summarize the main topics of the module, explaining why they are important	first day of the module	10–50 minutes
lecture	similar to what you would do in the classroom	early in the module	as needed, with breaks
lab session	demonstrate how to perform actions and supervise students carrying them out	any time during the module	30–90 minutes
module question-and-answer discussion	answer students' questions	middle/end of the module	15–60 minutes
small group problem-solving	students discuss and solve challenging problems	middle/end of the module	30–60 minutes
assignment-solution workshop	students present their solutions to the module's assignments and discuss them	after the assignment is due	20–30 minutes per assignment
module review	ask students if they have questions, summarize key topics, and ask students questions about the material	end of the module	30–60 minutes
term project presentation	students present their projects to classmates and faculty	near the end of the term	10–20 minutes per student
review for final exam	ask students if they have questions, then summarize the material that will be covered on the final exam and give examples of the level of detail that will be expected	a few days before the final exam	60–120 minutes

can also reassure the students that their questions are not stupid, while other students may chime in, saying that they too had a similar question.

Attendance at synchronous lectures should usually be optional. The ability of students to learn during synchronous online lectures declines fairly quickly, unless they're actively engaged by answering questions. Most synchronous sessions should be kept under an hour, and if they need to go longer, you should offer breaks.

Lab: Many courses have a lab component where students perform some synchronous hands-on activity. This activity might be a chemistry or electronics lab or a roleplay session in a social work course. The role of faculty may involve introducing the tools and techniques and supervising the activities. Labs make it possible to teach disciplines such as physical therapy, nursing, or music education online. Those activities can take place any time during a module and should usually be limited to 90 minutes.

Module Q&A session: Near the middle of each module, you should conduct a synchronous question-and-answer session where you invite students to ask questions. If they don't have many, it's a good idea for you to ask them how things are going. These sessions should usually take between 15 minutes and an hour, and it's occasionally helpful to have slides with diagrams or tables.

> Hint: If no one answers your questions, try to rephrase them or make them easier to answer. When you ask questions, be sure to allow plenty of time for students to think about their answers.

Small group problem-solving: Sometimes the best way to teach something is to have small groups of students work together synchronously to study or solve a problem. This has long been done on campus, and it can also be done online.

Provide a table for your students, listing time-slot options, and have them fill it out. Meeting scheduling websites online can do this for you, such as doodle.com or rallly.co. Break your students into groups based on when they can attend the sessions.

If your students are available at the same times throughout the term, you can ask them to sign up for weekly sessions. Ideally, faculty check in on these problem-solving sessions to see how things are going, to offer advice, or to provide additional problems; you'll find this easier if the sessions are at different times.

Assignment-solution workshops: Students often benefit from a synchronous session where they can present and talk about their solutions to assignments. These presentations often stimulate productive discussions, particularly if there are multiple solutions or points of view. These sessions should usually take 20 to 30 minutes per assignment, but they may go longer if things get interesting.

Module review: This helps cement the highlights of the module in your students' memory. You should identify the key points and the relationships between them. Present the material with the understanding that students have already studied it, to reinforce what they have learned. Slides can be helpful, because graphics are often a good way to summarize. You should encourage students to ask questions. Module review should take between 30 minutes and an hour.

Term project: If your course has a term project that counts as a significant fraction of the grade, we recommend that you require your students to present it to you and their classmates in a synchronous session where everyone can ask questions.

These synchronous sessions should be open to all faculty and students, and the topics of the presentations should be published on the course calendar, so interested students will know about them. In a course with TAs and many students, they may need to present at the same time in different **breakout rooms**. You should record these presentations so that students who are unable to attend can watch them.

The length of these term project presentations depends on the level of the course, how long it takes to communicate the key ideas, and its grading weight. In an undergraduate course the presentations should typically be no more than 20 minutes long, plus a few minutes for questions. In a graduate research course, they may be an hour long.

Final exam review: The review for the final exam should cover the most important material in the course, what students need to know for the exam and the types of questions in it. This review should demonstrate the level of detail you expect from your students in the final exam. For example, if you teach English grammar, you may review how to diagram a sentence, but you won't explain what an adverb is. The review can take an hour to two or more—with breaks, of course.

> Hint: You should always encourage your students to ask questions and take risks answering questions that they don't feel comfortable answering. You can do this by telling your students that you award extra credit for questions or answers that reveal things that they don't understand, because this helps other students who may well have the same question.

In synchronous sessions, students should present their ideas or solutions, with their classmates and faculty asking questions and commenting. It helps them learn, because they get immediate feedback. This also helps foster **academic integrity**, because students can only answer probing questions if they have done the work themselves. (For more on this, see Chapter 14.)

Appendix D
Creating and supervising asynchronous online discussions

This appendix describes how you should design the **asynchronous** discussions in your courses.

The initial posts in courses are often provided by faculty, as seed questions, and students respond to them with their own posts. Faculty-posed questions should be designed to keep conversations centered on learning objectives, to be open-ended, and to elicit insights that contribute to student understanding.

Discussions help students integrate and articulate what they're studying, and they should do most of the communicating. Asynchronous discussions allow students time to think about and research the questions and their replies to them. Students can participate without needing to be present at a particular time. Students may be able to communicate with each other better than they communicate with their faculty, and they can help each other learn the material. If a student responds to a faculty question with a post that is incomplete, other students may reply to the first post, providing the missing information.

Asynchronous discussions take the form of posts in the **LMS**, which can contain text, images, videos, or other HTML objects. Posts are organized into forums, and may be graded or ungraded. They can be viewed chronologically or threaded. If posts are viewed chronologically, they're presented in the order in which they're submitted. If they're viewed in a threaded format, each reply post is attached to its original; this preserves context and makes it easier to have multiple concurrent discussions.

Students participate in discussions when they enjoy them and feel that they are benefiting from them. They enjoy asynchronous discussions when:

- the questions posed are challenging and clearly relevant to what they're studying and their lives;
- answering the questions contributes to learning;
- they can discuss topics of interest to them;

- they can create posts that allow them to demonstrate their insights; and
- faculty are present in the discussions to provide insight.

Faculty can configure forums so that students have to respond to posts before they can see other responses. Posts can also be hidden until faculty want to reveal them, which makes it possible to have them "on deck," ready to use; faculty or TAs can reveal these hidden questions to invigorate discussions as they die down. Another advantage of keeping some questions in reserve is that it solves the problem of students who post later not having an opportunity to participate if earlier posters have exhausted the questions.

Discussion questions can also be posed by students. To keep the discussions on topic, we recommend that when a student initiates a thread, they cite the section in the readings for the **module** upon which it's based. For example, "In the reading in Chapter 6, the authors claim x, but I disagree because y." The advantages of this approach are that students are unlikely to run out of topics to discuss, and it gives them a chance to discuss what they want, while staying in scope.

Asynchronous discussion questions are usually developed along with the other asynchronous material. (For more on this, see Appendix A.) This allows faculty to improve them over time. When your course is over, go over the discussions carefully and identify the most successful questions: You're looking for ones that triggered a cascade of valuable replies.

We recommend that you create an asynchronous discussion forum for each module. Some courses benefit from forums that span all of the modules. For example, in a course with a term project there may be a forum to discuss it. All courses benefit from first-module forums where students introduce themselves ("Introduce Yourselves"), academic forums where students can post questions for faculty ("Ask the Faculty"), and forums for social interaction ("The Watercooler").

> Hint: Social interaction within programs works best if there are cross-course forums available, so that all students can communicate with each other, regardless of which course they may be in. These are useful places to post information about the program, success stories, and job openings in the field.

You can encourage your students to participate in asynchronous discussions by making them worth a significant part of their course grade. An appropriate discussion grading **rubric** will foster high-quality posts. Faculty should reward posts that contribute to learning. For example, a short question that stimulates a lot of pedagogically useful dialogue should rate a higher grade than a lengthy post that shuts down discussion or takes it off topic. (For more on creating grading rubrics, see Appendix G.) Module discussions should usually be graded. Social interaction forums should not be graded.

> Hint: The more you want students to participate in graded discussions, the more weight you should give that grade. Beware that if you weight discussions too heavily, some busy students may not be able to participate enough and will complain.

Faculty sometimes consider creating discussion forums on social media or other external sites, but we strongly discourage this. Some social media sites have many useful functions, but they lack faculty controls, an audit trail, security, and privacy. Faculty have no control over who can access or post to social media, nor can they delete offensive posts. This means bad actors may access students' posts and post themselves, hijacking a forum and potentially harassing students.

Faculty are responsible, however, for monitoring student activity in their courses. If a student's post violates the institution's code of conduct, faculty need an audit trail, a record of student activity that could be used in a hearing; social media sites do not provide this, but LMSs do. Furthermore, the Federal Educational Resource and Privacy Act provides protections for information shared in courses, but these protections do not apply to public forums (Timm & Duven, 2008).

Students do occasionally post things that violate student conduct policies, and faculty need to deal with this. In our experience, the most common inappropriate post in graded discussions is one that contains plagiarized material. If you have a hunch that something is wrong, you can run compilations of student posts through an **originality checker** to help catch plagiarized material. If a student plagiarizes in a post, faculty should usually email them the report from the originality checker, with an explanation that this is unacceptable. (For more on dealing with student misconduct, see Chapter 11.)

References

Timm, D. M., & Duven, C. J. (2008). Privacy and social networking sites. *New Directions for Student Services, 124,* 89–101.

Appendix E

Creating formative evaluations for asynchronous lectures

This appendix describes **formative evaluations** and how to create and use them. They give you an opportunity to provide your students with guidance that is specific to their needs, just as you would on campus.

Formative evaluation is an ungraded activity used to help students assess, or evaluate their mastery of material. Formative evaluations help students identify misunderstandings and misconceptions, and should provide immediate feedback that guides them to better understanding (Baleni, 2015). They should be given directly after presentation of material.

Formative evaluation allows faculty to engage with students indirectly, through pre-programmed interaction that they've written. We've had great success with an approach we call Test Yourself, in which a student is presented with questions embedded in **asynchronous** lectures; when they answer, they receive feedback which identifies the correct answer and provides tutorial material.

> Hint: When you're writing the feedback for an answer, imagine that your student had just given that answer in a classroom or one-on-one session, and write down what you would have said.

Students can use formative evaluations before or after they read an asynchronous lecture. For example, if they think they know the material, they can jump straight to the formative evaluation at the end of a section to test their knowledge. If they do well, they may skip the lecture, and continue to the next section. If they don't do well, they'll want to go back and study the lecture, knowing what they need to learn.

Students can also use formative evaluations after they read an asynchronous lecture. Taking them lets students know if they've learned the material and also identifies any area where they need more study. If they do well, it informs them that they can proceed confidently to the next material. If the students miss a question or two, the feedback will teach them what they need to learn. If they miss many questions, or don't even understand them, they need to go back to the lecture.

In an asynchronous lecture, formative evaluation can be implemented by using software that asks questions and provides immediate feedback. The evaluations may be embedded in lecture pages after each topic or take the form of practice tests after a **module**. Formative evaluations can also be embedded in videos with **in-video quizzing**, in which students are prompted to answer questions. The format you select will depend on the subject matter and technology you have available.

For example, every **LMS** offers the ability to make quizzes. You can use these as formative evaluations, but they usually require leaving the lecture page to go to the quiz. Embedding questions within asynchronous lecture pages takes extra effort and technology, but the immediacy of the feedback makes learning easier for your students, so ask your technical support people or **instructional designers** how you can do it.

If you can't embed them, you can link individual formative-evaluation quizzes to every page of your asynchronous lecture, but that means you'll have a lot of quizzes that don't count toward the final grade cluttering up your course grade book.

For the best results when configuring formative evaluations in your LMS, ensure that they:

- don't count toward grades;
- identify students in need of help;
- are short; they may contain only a single question;
- allow students to take them as often as they like;
- are automatically graded and released to students; and
- include extensive, tutorial feedback.

The usefulness of formative evaluation hinges on the quality of the questions and the feedback that you write. You should normally have a formative evaluation at the end of each topic. If you have one major topic per asynchronous lecture page, you should have a formative evaluation at the bottom of each page, covering the key points of the topic. We have found that **multiple-answer questions** provide better coverage than **multiple-choice questions**. They also let you assess subtler aspects of the topic. For example, you can describe a scenario and then ask which of the following statements about it are true.

> Hint: Many question types, such as essays and short answers, don't work well as formative evaluations because it's technically difficult to grade them automatically and provide appropriate feedback.

Formative evaluations can help you improve both your **synchronous** and asynchronous lectures. If your students consistently struggle with a particular formative evaluation question, you know that the lecture hasn't prepared them for it and you should strengthen the lecture (Peterson, 2016). Formative evaluations can also give you information about struggling students. If you use built-in LMS quizzes, you can get this information from the grade book. If you use quizzes that aren't in the LMS, you can check written reports their software provides.

> Hint: If many students struggle with a particular formative evaluation in an asynchronous lecture, you should try to cover the material in a synchronous lecture, so students have another chance to ask questions.

References

Baleni, Z. G. (2015). Online formative assessment in higher education: Its pros and cons. *Electronic Journal of e-Learning*, 13(4), 228–236.

Peterson, J. L. (2016). Formative evaluations in online classes. *Journal of Educators Online*, 13(1), 1–24.

Appendix F

Creating and updating tests in your LMS

When you're designing a new test that will be given via an **LMS**, the basic process is similar to devising a test that's administered on campus. Begin by identifying the topics that you want to assess, and be careful that the answers don't require material that you haven't covered yet. Look at the topics and see if you can easily design questions that cover more than one.

You'll also need to decide how many questions you want to have. If a test has too few questions, students may get poor grades if they miss just one. You can reduce this problem by choosing question types that support partial credit, such as essay and **multiple-answer** ("checkbox") types. For automatically graded tests, we've found that about 20 questions works well.

One of the biggest advantages of tests implemented in an LMS is automatic grading, and you'll need to decide when to use it. Many faculty who are new to creating online tests start by trying to create automatically graded questions, and if they can't devise one that assesses what they want, they create a manually graded question. Faculty with more experience in creating online tests usually use only automatically graded questions.

The most common automatically graded questions are multiple choice and multiple answer. A **multiple-choice question** allows only one answer ("radio buttons"), whereas multiple-answer questions allow more than one answer to be selected ("checkboxes"). Multiple-answer questions often take the forms of "Select all that are true about..." versus "Which one of the following is the best..." A multiple-answer question typically gives partial credit for every right answer (and penalizes incorrect answers), whereas a multiple-choice question is all-or-nothing based on the single answer.

Most faculty use multiple-choice questions because they've always been easy to create and score. Multiple-answer questions are less familiar, but they have many advantages; they support partial credit, and they can cover more material, so you don't need as many questions. You can pose a complex problem, such as a patient's lab results, and probe the students' understanding of their medical implications, without students needing to read a separate problem for each answer. This lets you ask more nuanced questions without taking more of your students' time.

The main problem with multiple-answer questions in manually graded tests is that there's a fair amount of arithmetic required to grade each question. The LMS does the grading for us, so we gain the advantages of these questions without increasing the grading workload.

It's important that you penalize students for selecting incorrect responses in multiple-answer questions, or clever students may realize that there's no penalty for getting a wrong answer and check every box to get a perfect score. To prevent this, you need to put a negative number value for the wrong answers. We have found that a weight of -15 percent is sufficient to discourage this without distorting the grading.

As with **formative evaluations**, when you're writing test questions, be sure to provide feedback for all answers. For example, if a multiple-answer question has five options, you should write a sentence or two for each answer, explaining if it should be selected or not and why. It takes some effort, but it helps improve the quality of the questions, and it almost completely eliminates the time you'll need to spend answering student questions about the tests or reviewing them in **synchronous** sessions.

Some faculty think that automatic grading can only cover rudimentary topics, but there are techniques for creating good, automatically graded questions at all levels (Geigle, Zhai, & Ferguson, 2016, pp. Scale, 351–360). For example, one of the authors uses automatically graded, multiple-answer questions in his graduate-level courses, where he poses a business scenario and then asks which of the options describes significant risks and appropriate management actions.

You can also create automatically graded questions that have images, graphics, or videos. To do this, pose a question for which the answer is a graphic and ask your students to choose the ones which are appropriate. For example, you can show students images of leaves and ask which ones are oak, or show dissected kidneys and ask students to identify the images that have evidence of nephritis.

> Hint: Be careful not to have the image filenames or **alt attributes** give away the answers!

Automatic grading does have significant limitations, including an inability to handle essay questions; artificial intelligence technology can't yet handle the wide range of ideas that may be in an essay.

In addition, your LMS may or may not be able to handle automatically graded questions where the answer is a word or phrase. Before you use a question of this type, assuming it will be graded correctly automatically, you should test your LMS's grading of such questions with representative variations of what students type. Some LMSs can't recognize correct answers if they differ from the answer you provided in minor ways, such as plurals, tense changes, or spelling errors. For example, if you are expecting an answer "first normal form," but students type "1st normal form," your LMS might mark it wrong. You can avoid this issue by posing short-answer questions as multiple-choice or multiple-answer questions, which your LMS can grade correctly.

Another advantage of fully automatically graded tests is that you can set them up to be returned to students as soon as they're submitted, providing immediate feedback. However, immediately released tests can undermine **academic integrity** if students who take the test earlier share the results with students who haven't taken it yet. You can overcome this by constructing your tests to have questions randomly selected from question sets.

You should randomize both the question selection and the answer order. Random question selection does require that you write more questions and organize them into question sets. (For more on question randomization, see Chapter 14.) This is more work initially, but it will increase the lifetime and integrity of your test. We urge you to take your test yourself, before your students do, to catch any errors before your students see them. If you have TAs, and the test is new or substantially updated, you should have a TA take it too, because they'll probably notice different things than you do.

After students have taken a test, examine the mean and **discriminant** statistics of each question to verify that they're measuring what you want them to. The mean is the average score. If all of your students earn perfect scores on a question, it confirms that they've all met the learning objectives, but it won't help you identify students who need additional study on that topic. If few of your students get a question right, then you know they didn't learn that topic well, as measured by that question, so you may need to cover it again. What you're aiming for are questions of moderate difficulty, as measured by your grading goals. Your students should find them challenging, but not daunting. Table F.1 summarizes mean score ranges for typical grading standards, and what to do in each case.

The discriminant is a way to study the differences between two or more groups (Klecka, 1980), such as how well a question differentiates between students with different levels of understanding (Asuero et al., 2006). The discriminant is a number between -1 and 1 that measures how well scores on a question correlate with scores on the test as a whole. Different LMSs calculate the discriminant differently. For example, Blackboard Ultra

Table F.1 Mean score ranges and what to do in each case

Mean score range	Implication	What to do before releasing results to students	What to do when updating the test
>90%	Too easy	Nothing	Make it more challenging
70% to 90%	About right	Nothing	Nothing
30% to 70%	A little too challenging	Nothing	Evaluate ways to improve coverage or make the question a little easier
<30%	Too challenging	Nothing	Improve coverage of this area; make the question easier

calculates the discriminant as the Pearson correlation coefficient between the scores on a question and the scores on the **assessment** (Blackboard, 2021). Regardless of how the discriminant is calculated, it is interpreted similarly.

A question with a discriminant of zero is one where the better and weaker students scored the same. A discriminant of 1 indicates that scores on the question are a perfect predictor of how well students did on the test as a whole. A discriminant of -1 predicts that students who did well on the question did poorly on the test, and those who did poorly on the question did well on the test. Questions with negative discriminants reduce the validity of the tests of which they are a part.

Table F.2 lists ranges of the discriminant, what they indicate, and how faculty can respond when releasing and updating the test.

High discriminants help faculty identify questions that some students get wrong, even though they have good understanding of the material the question assesses. Surprisingly, a discriminant can be too high. One of the authors developed a test where many of the questions had discriminants of 100 percent, which demoralized students who understood the material fairly well, but not well enough to get any credit on these questions. He replaced those questions.

After your students have taken a test, and you have examined the score statistics, you should identify test questions that don't accurately measure student understanding. For example, the statistics may not be accurate if not enough students have taken a particular question. (If questions are drawn randomly from a question set, the number of times they are used will vary.) You can also look at a question by examining the answers of the best students, to see what they got wrong. This will usually reveal a problem, if there is one.

A question with a discriminant of zero doesn't tell faculty how well students understood the assessed subject matter. A question with a negative

Table F.2 Discriminant ranges and what to do in each case

Discriminant range	Implication	What to do before releasing results to students	What to do when updating the test
-1 to 0	Something is wrong with the question	Attempt to recover; see methods below. If you can't recover, zero the weight for the question.	Correct or replace the question.
0 to 0.1	Weak discrimination	Nothing	Improve or replace question.
Between 0.1 and 0.3	Mediocre discrimination	Nothing	Change or replace the question.
0.3 to 0.9	Good discrimination	Nothing	Nothing
0.9 to 1	Excellent discrimination	Nothing	If there are many questions with very high discriminants in the test, see the note below.

discriminant has a serious problem, which should be addressed. This can happen if a question has different interpretations, and students with good understanding interpret it in a way that faculty didn't expect.

> Hint: How students answer a question is a measure of their interaction with the question, which is a test of both the students and the question itself.

The way that you correct errors that you made in setting up questions depends on the type of question and the kind of error. Common sources of errors are incorrect answers that you provided when you created the question, and incorrect weights that you gave to multiple-answer questions.

Table F.3 summarizes common errors in test setup and ways to correct them.

One of the advantages of multiple-answer questions is that the most common problems are with one answer; you can usually fix these problems by zeroing the weight of that answer. Because it's difficult to create test questions that are interpreted the way that you expect them to be by all students, we recommend that you use new questions in formative evaluations or practice quizzes for one or two terms before you put them in tests that

Table F.3 Common errors in test setup and ways to correct them

Question type	Error type	Ways to correct them
True/False	Incorrect question answer	Correct the answer and have the LMS recalculate the scores.
True/False	Question has multiple interpretations with different answers	Zero the weight of this question in the test.
Multiple choice	Incorrect question answer	Correct the answer and have the LMS recalculate the scores.
Multiple choice	Question has multiple interpretations with different acceptable answers	Zero the weight of this question in the test.
Multiple answer	Incorrect question answer(s)	Correct the answer(s) and have the LMS recalculate the scores.
Multiple answer	Question has multiple interpretations with different answers	Analyze the statistics for the selected answers and identify any with negative discriminants; zero the weights of these answers, recompute the statistics, and see if the discriminant is positive. If this doesn't work, zero the weight of the question in the test.
Short answer	Students provide unexpected answers	If it's automatically graded by the LMS, correct the question's range of acceptable answers and recompute the scores. Grade them manually if necessary.
Essay	Question has multiple interpretations	Update the **rubrics** and regrade the question.

count. Also note that sometimes you may need to manually grade at least some of the submissions. You should continue to analyze the statistics and improve your questions from term to term.

References

Asuero, A. G., Sayago, A., & González, A. G. (2006). The correlation coefficient: An overview. *Critical Reviews in Analytical Chemistry*, *36*(1), 41–59.

Blackboard. (2021). Question Analysis. Retrieved July 28, 2021, from https://help.blackboard.com/Learn/Instructor/Ultra/Tests_Pools_Surveys/Item_Analysis.

Geigle, C., Zhai, C., & Ferguson, D. C. (2016). *An exploration of automated grading of complex assignments.* Proceedings from the Third ACM Conference on Learning@ Scale.

Klecka, W. R. (1980). *Discriminant analysis* (19). Beverly Hills: Sage Publications.

Appendix G

Creating grading rubrics

A **rubric** is a document that defines how a graded student submission is scored (Barkley & Major, 2016; Reddy & Andrade, 2010). Faculty who grade everything themselves may think that they don't need rubrics, but they should provide them anyway, so that their students know what is expected and how their work will be graded. If faculty use graders or TAs, rubrics are essential to assure fair, consistent, and correct grading.

Grading rubrics should be aligned with your learning objectives. They should reward evidence of learning and, occasionally, contributions to other students' learning. The overall framework for grading is defined in the syllabus and the grading for individual items is in the rubrics. The scope of rubrics should be individual graded items, with no mention of how those items affect course grades.

The place for rubrics in a course depends on their scope. If you have a rubric that applies to all of the assignments in a course, it's appropriate to put it in the syllabus. If you have a rubric for a term project, it is appropriate to put it with documents related to the project. In general, the rubric should be in a place where students will see it when they're working on the assignment. You should link to rubrics rather than duplicating them, because they are frequently edited and they need to be consistent.

Rubrics often begin with statements of what you want your students to learn. Different **learning activities** may have different goals for the same subject matter; for example, an assignment may have a learning objective of helping students practice what they've studied, while a discussion may have an objective of having students articulate what they have studied.

Rubrics should be designed to reflect the purpose of the learning activities and should specify how you'll measure the quality of students' submissions. Rubrics may depend on the subject matter, because different disciplines have different ways of evaluating the quality of work. For example, a painting submitted in an art class may be scored based on composition, while a proof submitted in a math class may be graded based on its correct use of established proof methods. They also depend on the type of submission; for example, rubrics for discussions may be very different than rubrics for research papers.

When you expect that your students may have trouble understanding a rubric, include annotated examples of submissions with different grades.

In some courses, a single rubric can cover more than one submission, while in other courses it may be necessary to have multiple rubrics. For example, a management course may have one rubric for essay assignments and another for problem-solving assignments. The essay rubric might specify that certain percentages of the scores are based on the content and exposition, while the problem-solving rubric might specify that scores are based on the quality of the solution and how well it's expressed. Table G.1 demonstrates a rubric that covers all of the assignments in a course.

Rubrics for problem-solving assignments and essays are usually fairly easy to define, but rubrics for discussions and class contributions may not be as

Table G.1 Assignment grading rubric

All assignment submissions are evaluated on the quality of the original content, and on how well the content is expressed.

Grade	Content (70%)	Exposition (30%)
A+	The content demonstrates exceptional understanding of all relevant topics. All issues are thoroughly covered, and all content is relevant. No technical or coverage errors are present.	The presentation of all ideas and designs is exceptionally clear and persuasive; the entire submission is exceptionally well organized.
A	The content demonstrates strong understanding of all relevant topics. All issues are thoroughly covered, and all content is relevant. Minor technical or coverage errors may be present.	The presentation of all ideas and designs is exceptionally clear and persuasive; there are a few ways to improve the clarity or organization of the submission.
A−	The content demonstrates understanding of all relevant topics. All issues are thoroughly covered, and all content is relevant.	The presentation of all ideas and designs is very clear and persuasive. There are many ways to improve the clarity or organization of the submission.
B+	The content demonstrates some understanding of all relevant topics. Almost all major relevant issues are covered, and the content is reasonably on topic.	The presentation of all ideas and designs is clear and persuasive. The clarity and organization of the submission could be improved.
B	The content demonstrates understanding of most relevant topics. Most major relevant issues are covered, and all content is reasonably on topic.	The presentation of most ideas and designs is clear and persuasive. The clarity and organization of the submission could be significantly improved.

(continued)

Table G.1 (Cont.)

Grade	Content (70%)	Exposition (30%)
B−	The content demonstrates understanding of most relevant topics. There is acceptable coverage of major relevant issues, and the content is reasonably on topic.	The presentation of most ideas and designs is generally clear. The clarity and organization of the submission are below expectations.
C+	The content demonstrates moderate understanding of relevant topics. Some major relevant issues are covered, and some content is on topic.	Some parts of the submission are hard to understand. The clarity and organization of the submission are substantially below expectations.
C	The content demonstrates some understanding of some of the relevant topics. Some major relevant issues are covered, and a portion of the content is on topic.	About half of the submission is hard to understand; about half is disorganized. Much improvement is needed in the clarity and exposition.
C−	The content demonstrates little understanding of the relevant topics. Only a few of the major relevant issues are covered. The focus of the content may be off topic or on secondary topics.	Most parts of the submission are hard to understand. The submission appears sloppily organized and written.
D	The content demonstrates almost no understanding of or insight into the relevant topics. Few of the major relevant issues are covered, and the content may be largely off-topic.	Almost all of the submission is disorganized and hard to understand. The writing is so poor that it's hard to grade the content.
F	The content demonstrates no understanding of or insight into the relevant topics. No major relevant issues are covered, and the content is entirely off-topic.	The entire submission is disorganized and hard to understand. The writing is so poor that it's nearly impossible to grade the content.

obvious. The learning objectives of discussions are helping students learn to articulate what they are studying and identifying areas where they need additional study. It's important to keep the rubrics tightly aligned with these objectives, because some seemingly obvious ideas are traps. For example, rubrics which simply require students to post frequently don't work well, because they result in many posts with little pedagogic value. Rewarding students for the lengths of their posts often results in rambling posts that waste their classmates' time. What you want are posts that contribute to learning. A short post that asks a good leading question, aligned with the learning objectives, may stimulate many response posts; these are ideal. One way you can do this is with a peer grading system, in which students rate each of their classmates' posts.

The level of detail of a rubric varies with the educational level of the course. Rubrics for an introductory course may specify everything. However, this approach doesn't work well in advanced graduate courses, in which students have a great deal of freedom in what they explore and how they do it; more flexible rubrics are needed, that place more responsibility on faculty. Table G.2 is an example of a rubric used in an introductory course.

By contrast, the paragraph below is an example of a rubric used in a PhD-level research course:

> Your discussions for each **module** will be assigned a numeric score following the score-to-grade correspondence in the syllabus. Your scores will be based on how much they contribute to your classmates' learning. Good discussion posts will stimulate your classmates to think deeply about the subject and respond insightfully. Discussion posts that merely parrot what is obvious or agree with prior posts will not earn good scores. Discussion posts that discourage further discussion do not contribute to learning. Discussion posts that lead the discussion off topic may waste your classmates' time.

In some courses active student participation helps students learn the skills spelled out in the learning objectives, so students should be graded for participation. Students can participate in these courses **synchronously** or **asynchronously**, and you can grade these separately. For example, in law or social work courses students need to master verbal communication skills specific to these professions, and they should have an opportunity to practice these and be graded on them in synchronous sessions. In other courses students may participate synchronously or asynchronously, and you may be able to grade these together. Table G.3 provides an example of an asynchronous class-participation rubric.

Group projects are important for teaching students how to work as members of teams. Grading group projects requires that you can tell what each student contributed. The easiest way to do this is to design the project so that individual students are responsible for gradable deliverables. If your groups make graded presentations, you should have each student present the portion of the work they did.

Sometimes a project needs a final report or research paper which incorporates contributions from many students; in these cases, you can require that the students each write chapters or sections of the report, and the authorship should be indicated in the report. One or a few students will usually assume leadership roles for a project, and they can get credit for it if you include leadership components in the project grading.

Table G.2 Example of a discussion grading rubric for an introductory course

Criteria	65–69	70–79	80–89	90–94	95–100
Participation	Very limited participation	Participation generally lacks frequency or relevance	Reasonably useful, relevant participation during the discussion period	Frequently relevant and consistent participation throughout the discussion period	Continually relevant and consistent participation throughout the discussion period
Community	Mostly indifferent to discussion	Little effort to keep discussions going or provide help	Reasonable effort to respond thoughtfully, provide help, and/or keep discussions going	Often responds thoughtfully, in a way that frequently keeps discussions going and provides help	Continually responds thoughtfully, in a way that consistently keeps discussions going and provides help
Content	No useful, on-topic, or interesting information, ideas, or analysis	Hardly any useful, on-topic, or interesting information, ideas, or analysis	Reasonably useful, on-topic, and interesting information, ideas, and/or analysis	Frequently useful, on-topic, and interesting information, ideas, and analysis	Exceptionally useful, on-topic, and interesting information, ideas, and analysis
Reflection and Synthesis	No significant effort to clarify, summarize, or synthesize topics that have been discussed			Contributes to group's effort to clarify, summarize, or synthesize topics that have been discussed	Leads group's effort to clarify, summarize, or synthesize topics that have been discussed

Table G.3 Example of an asynchronous class-participation rubric

	F	D	C	B	A
Participation and alignment with learning objectives	Doesn't participate sufficiently, never on topic	Contributes sporadically, rarely on topic	Contributes occasionally, sometimes on topic	Contributes frequently, usually on topic	Contributes frequently, always on topic
Community	Discourages others from joining the discussions. Attacks other students' posts	Ignores other students' posts in the discussions and discourages follow-up posts. Doesn't support those who are already in the conversation	Responds to openings in the discussions, but doesn't try to draw in others. Occasionally supports those who are already in the conversation	Usually creates openings for others to join the discussions and draws in some other students. Often supports those who are already in the conversation	Actively encourages others to join the discussions by creating openings and replying affirmatively to posts, drawing many others into the conversation. Actively supports those who are already in the conversation
Posting quality	Lacks insight. Fails to contribute to learning. Rambling and incomprehensible.	Rarely insightful. Rarely contributes to learning. Rarely succinct or clear.	Occasionally insightful. Occasionally contributes to learning. Sometimes succinct and clear.	Usually insightful. Usually contributes to learning. Usually succinct and clear.	Always insightful. Always contributes to learning. Always succinct and clear.

(continued)

Table G.3 (Cont.)

	F	D	C	B	A
Content	Posts are plagiarized. Distributes misinformation that undermines learning.	Poor-quality contributions that waste everyone's time. Expresses opinions without evidence.	Sometimes provides meaningful, constructive comments that move the discussion forward. Expresses opinions with weak evidence. Adds alternative points of view that confuse people.	Usually provides meaningful, constructive comments that move the discussion forward. Supports positions with evidence from the required readings. Occasionally adds alternative points of view that help people learn.	Provides meaningful, constructive comments that provide insight and move the discussion forward. Supports positions with evidence from outside research. Frequently adds alternative points of view that help people learn.

References

Barkley, E. F., & Major, C. H. (2016). *Learning assessment techniques: A handbook for college faculty.* John Wiley & Sons.

Reddy, Y. M., & Andrade, H. (2010). A review of rubric use in higher education. *Assessment & Evaluation in Higher Education, 35*(4), 435–448.

Appendix H

Managing audio for synchronous sessions

Your **synchronous** sessions will be more successful if your students can talk with each other and with you, as opposed to you just making an uninterrupted speech. This requires stable, low-noise audio, so you'll need to manage background noise, audio feedback, and other acoustic challenges.

Sounds that are near a microphone are picked up much more loudly than sounds at a distance, so even the crinkling of a snack wrapper can be surprisingly loud. We recommend that everyone use headsets. If you're wearing a headset with a noise-canceling microphone, you can open a bag of potato chips without disturbing the whole class. One of the authors taught online successfully with a headset while construction workers were jackhammering next door, and his students couldn't hear the noise. If you wear a headset, you'll also be able to hear your students more clearly; this is particularly important if they have lots of background noise, poor microphones, or unfamiliar accents.

The distance between the speaker's mouth and the microphone dramatically changes the volume, so if you turn your head away from your microphone, your students may not be able to hear you. To make sure that all students can hear you clearly, you should wear a microphone, which can be either a headset or a **lavalier** microphone. The main advantage of lavalier microphones over stationary microphones is that they are attached to the user, so volume varies less. Headset microphones are near your mouth, so they pick up much less background noise.

How you manage the students talking depends on how many students you have in your synchronous session. There are three possible strategies:

- Open microphone: If you have meetings of 10 or fewer people with good microphone discipline, everyone can have their microphones on and there will be little talking over one another. With small classes or disciplined students, it works well to begin with an open microphone, so students who are in the **virtual room** early can talk with you and

each other. If there are issues with background noise or feedback, you or your students need to mute their microphones. For example, if a student has a child talking in the background, you can mute their microphone.
- Initial mute, but can later unmute: With larger groups, all of the background noises add up, so it's easier to start a meeting with all students muted and have them unmute themselves when they have a question or something to say. We've successfully used this strategy with 100 graduate students, who wore headsets and had a lot of experience online.
- Keep them muted: This is primarily used in lectures when there are so many students that the audio noise becomes unmanageable, and for lectures in which you want students to post questions in a chat window. Your students can let you know when they want you to unmute them by using the **videoconferencing** system's **"raise your hand"** function.

If some of your students are on campus with you while others are online, it can be challenging for faculty to divide their attention between these two groups. Typically, faculty fail to notice when an online student wants to say something or has a question; you need to make an extra effort to scan the screen for these "raised hands." Another approach is to have a TA or student in the classroom, monitoring the chat, who lets you know about student questions.

> Hint: If you use a headset in a classroom, it may interfere with your ability to hear students in the room with you. You can overcome this by using only one earpiece.

Appendix I

Dealing with technology problems during class

Technical problems can and do arise while we are teaching. Table I.1 lists common technical problems and what faculty can do to overcome them or minimize their impact.

Table I.1 Common technical problems and what you can do about them

What's not working	What you can do
Something isn't working on your device	You can determine whether the problem is with your computer or somewhere else by attempting the same operation using a different device.
A slow or erratic internet connection	You can measure the speed of your internet connection using a web tool. If your connection is slower than about 20 Mb/sec, you may want to speak with your internet service provider or tech support. Slow internet connections are more common in the evening, when people are often streaming video. Because video uses lots of **bandwidth**, if you are using **videoconferencing**, try turning off your video. If you're using Wi-Fi, you may be able to change to a different network. If you're connected via Ethernet, you can try connecting through Wi-Fi.
Synchronous- session video breaks up or fails	This can be due to a slow or erratic internet connection. Use a static image instead of the video from your webcam.
Videoconferencing system crashes or hangs up	Quit and relaunch the videoconferencing system application. If the videoconferencing application complains about inadequate resources, check that no other applications are running. If it still crashes, your internet connection is almost certainly the problem. You can confirm this by trying a different videoconferencing program.
Your internet connection fails	Change internet connections if you can. If this doesn't work, use your cell phone as a hot spot. If this doesn't work, use your cell phone to send your students an announcement that you'll be rescheduling, and asking them to email you with any urgent issues.

Table I.1 (Cont.)

What's not working	What you can do
The **LMS** crashes or becomes unusably slow	Email your students from outside the LMS, letting them know that you're aware of the problem, and asking them to email you with any urgent issues. If your synchronous-session server is still working, let your students know that you'll be there for them at specific times. If the problem persists for a long time, consider emailing your students the lecture content, increasing the number of synchronous sessions, and temporarily moving the **asynchronous** discussions to another website that can support them.
Broken link in your course website	Fix the link or send an announcement providing your students with either the correct link or its content.
A video not playing for you	Try another browser. If this doesn't fix it, try another device, such as your phone or tablet. If this doesn't work, contact tech support.
A video not playing for some students, but it is for you	Tell your students to try using one of the browsers approved for the course; tell them which browser works for you.

Glossary

academic integrity Policies and procedures that aim to assure that the grades and credit that students receive for their coursework accurately represent their learning in the program.
accessibility The extent to which a course can be used by anyone, regardless of disability or impairment. See universal design.
add-ons Software modules that can be added to an LMS to provide additional functionality.
alt attribute An attribute that may be present in any HTML element that specifies text to be displayed when the element cannot be used in its primary form. For example, a screen reader used by a blind student is unable to describe an image, but it can read the alt attribute that has been assigned to said image.
answer coding The indication of the correct answers and their weights in a test.
APA style References and inline citations formatted according to the rules of the American Psychological Association Publication Manual.
assessment Something that helps faculty determine how well individual students have met the course learning objectives. Common assessments include quizzes, tests, exams, graded assignments, and graded discussions.
assessment, formative See formative evaluation.
assessment, summative See summative assessment.
asynchronous interaction Communication that is not in real time, such as written lectures or email, where students and faculty are not engaged at the same time.
augmented reality Technology that allows digital content to overlay actual visuals and audio.
blended Courses where some of the teaching takes place on campus and some online. See also flipped courses.
breakout room A videoconferencing meeting room that is used for small groups, broken off from the main (default) meeting room.

CART (Communication Access Real-time Translation) Services create transcriptions of synchronous activities while they are running.

course map A document listing the modules of a course, including their learning objectives, topics, learning objects, assessments, and assignments, used for planning a course before it's developed or revised. A course map is usually a compilation of module maps.

curriculum The courses that are available for students to take in a program. A curriculum may support multiple courses of study.

development The process by which courses are produced for students to take. Development usually precedes course launch, though some development may be done while a course is running.

discriminant A measure of how well an assessment differentiates between students with different levels of understanding, commonly expressed as a percentage.

document camera A digital camera mounted on a stand, used to present documents or things you're writing or drawing.

embedded objects Images, videos, illustrations, self-assessments, interactive and other learning objects that are presented on a website page.

engagement A property of successful learning activities which encourages students to reflect on, work with, or feel connected to the subject matter.

flipped courses Courses in which students study the course material using digital technology to prepare for class sessions. They spend class time in discussions, group problem-solving, lab exercises, and other activities that work best in an on-campus classroom, rather than listening to lectures.

formative evaluation An activity used to help students evaluate their mastery of material while they are learning, which does not count toward their grade. It should be given directly after presentation of material and provide immediate feedback, to correct misunderstandings and misconceptions. Examples include faculty asking students a question in class and providing feedback, or practice tests.

gamification Introducing game-like elements to increase students' attention.

grade begging Asking for extra credit to earn a higher grade, disputing scores for graded items, and other things that students do to try to improve their scores and grades.

high touch Courses or programs in which students have many opportunities to interact with their faculty.

hybrid See blended.

in-video quizzing A video that includes embedded questions. Some use the student's answer to either continue playing the video or go back to where the material was covered.

incomplete A grade assigned to students to allow them and their faculty additional time to complete the course. Incompletes may be offered by faculty due to student illness or other good reasons, provided that most of the coursework has been completed.

instructional designer A person who helps develop, organize, and implement instructional materials to make them more effective, usable, accessible, or available online.

interactive objects Learning objects that respond to student interaction.

lavalier microphone A small microphone that attaches to clothing.

learning activities Things that students do to learn the material. These may include reading, watching videos, interacting with multimedia objects, engaging in synchronous or asynchronous discussions and study groups with faculty and classmates, and completing assignments, assessments, and projects.

Learning Management System (LMS) A computer server that hosts the websites for online courses, including grade books, lectures, assessments, and assignments. An LMS may host multimedia, video, or other services, or they may be hosted separately and linked from the LMS.

learning object A digital entity used for education or training, such as text, embedded images, videos, illustrations, simulations, self-assessments, or tests. See interactive objects.

lockdown browser Software that temporarily disables many functions on a student's computer while they access an online test. When using a lockdown browser, they're unable to open another URL, print, copy, or access other applications until they have submitted the test.

LMS See Learning Management System.

low touch Courses or programs in which students don't have many opportunities to interact with their faculty.

module A coordinated collection of learning objects that students study together, commonly in one week. Although it is often used interchangeably with "week," the generic term allows the same course to be used in different length terms.

Module 0: Prerequisite Review A review module in an asynchronous online course that primes students for the course, but does not count toward students' grades. This material may come from prerequisite courses, and, if possible, should be made available before the course launches.

module map A document listing the learning objectives, topics, learning activities, learning objects, assessments, and assignments to be included in a specific unit of a course, used for planning the development or revision of a module.

MOOC (Massive Open Online Course) An online course designed to have unlimited enrollment.

multiple-answer question A question format in which students select all of the answer options that are true.

multiple-choice question A question format in which students select the single best answer.

network bandwidth The rate at which a computer network can transmit information; network speed is mainly important for videos and videoconferencing.

originality checker A software system that compares student submissions to large databases of published works and prior student submissions, to verify that the work is original.

outcome analysis Assessments of how well educational programs meet students' needs, program learning objectives, and employer needs.

"raise your hand" function A feature of videoconferencing systems that allows participants to signal that they would like to speak, much as they would by raising their hand in an on-campus classroom.

rubric Instructions to students and graders specifying how a graded item is to be scored.

sandbox A computer environment in which users can experiment without risk. One example is a course website that is not accessible by students, but can be used by faculty and staff who are experimenting with new technologies and teaching techniques.

screen readers Software that reads the text displayed on a computer screen using a speech synthesizer or Braille display.

student evaluations Questionnaires completed by students evaluating the course, faculty, and technologies. These are useful for evaluating course quality and planning course updates.

study group Students who meet synchronously to help each other learn. Study groups may be facilitated by faculty.

study guide A table listing things that students need to do, and when they're due. Guides may recommend that students do things in a certain order, such as read a textbook chapter before that module's asynchronous lecture.

study room A virtual meeting room that supports study groups. A study room may include synchronous multimedia as well as asynchronous activities, such as discussions. A study room may be accessible to all students in a course, to the students in a group, or only to students with an affinity, such as a time zone or interest. See virtual room.

summative assessment An activity used to help students assess their mastery of material after they have learned it, and which counts toward their grade. Common examples include quizzes, tests, and exams.

synchronous interaction Communication that is in real time, such as videoconferencing, where students and faculty are engaged at the same time.

telepresence Situations in which students or faculty participate in a classroom setting, using technology, even though they are not physically present in the classroom. Also commonly known as remote learning.

transition course(s) Courses designed to prepare students without adequate preparation for advanced study, commonly used to prepare graduate students for study in an area that they have not studied as undergraduates.

universal design Course and software design that helps all students, including those with disabilities. See accessibility.

videoconferencing Software that lets people communicate with video and voice, commonly used for synchronous teaching.

virtual reality Software and hardware that give the user the feeling or sense that they are in a different place. For example, a student can see functions of a computer program represented as building blocks.

virtual room A space for synchronous meetings, implemented using technology such as Adobe Connect, Blackboard Collaborate, or Zoom. Virtual rooms may be used for synchronous class sessions led by the faculty, one-on-one sessions between faculty and students, student presentations, study groups, or other situations where synchronous communication is best. See study room.

welcome emails Emails that faculty send to their enrolled students before the course opens, welcoming them to the course and guiding them in preparing for it.

wiki A website that supports collaborative editing of its content by its users.

Zoom room Named after the Zoom software, this can refer to either a virtual space or breakout room provided by the videoconferencing system or a physical room in which someone uses a videoconferencing system, which can often be seen in the background of the videoconference user.

Printed in the United States
by Baker & Taylor Publisher Services